BERLIN
teils teils

Die Quadriga auf dem Brandenburger Tor

The Quadriga on the Brandenburg Gate

Deutsche Verlags-Anstalt
Stuttgart

©1972 Deutsche Verlags-Anstalt GmbH, Stuttgart
Titel und Grafik-Design, Beratung: Manfred Glemser, Stuttgart
Idee und Konzeption: Ludwig Windstoßer, Stuttgart
Aufnahmen: Kodacolor-X Film
Farbvergrößerungen: Kodak Ektacolor Papier
English translation: Paul Moor
Gesamtherstellung:
Deutsche Verlags-Anstalt
Grafischer Großbetrieb, Stuttgart
Printed in Germany
ISBN 3 421 01605 4

Ludwig Windstoßer
Photo

Thilo Koch
Text

BERLIN
teils teils

BERLIN
BERLIN BERLIN

Mit einem kleinen „Naja"

Sag, was bist du, Berlin.
Sag mir's auf deine Art:
mit Selbstironie,
bißchen schnoddrig, bißchen sentimental,
realistisch, optimistisch, trocken –
mit diesem kleinen Naja
hinter jedem großen Satz.

Was möchten Sie denn hören?
Wir halten da eine ganze Kollektion
von prima Schlagzeilen feil:
Freie Stadt Westberlin,
Drehscheibe zwischen Ost und West,
Stadt der Begegnungen,
Las Vegas im Roten Meer,
Schaufenster des Westens,
Besondere politische Einheit,
Frontstadt,
Vorposten der Freiheit.
Wollen wir nicht zur Abwechslung
mal alle Berlin-Klischees
beiseite lassen?
Oder ist das auch schon wieder 'n Klischee?
Sehen Sie,
das Schwierige mit Berlin ist:
von alledem stimmt schon was,
aber das Gegenteil ist auch wahr.
Wenn Sie mich ganz persönlich fragen,
dann frage ich Sie zurück:
Warum eigentlich soll Berlin,
West-Berlin meine ich,
denn immer eine besondere Aufgabe haben?
Besondere Aufgaben hatten wir genug.
Nun sind wir pensioniert
von der Geschichte –
als Reichshauptstadt sowieso,
aber auch als
Vorposten,
Frontstadt,
Schaufenster,
Drehscheibe.
Und wenn man so viel Geschichte
gemacht hat, mitgemacht hat
wie Berlin,
dann läßt man ganz gerne
mal anderen den Vortritt –
denen drüben zum Beispiel,
in der Hauptstadt der DDR.

Teils teils –
da haben Sie, finde ich,
dieses ganze Berlin,
das heute nun mal immer nur
'n halbes Berlin ist –
von wo aus Sie auch die Sache betrachten:
Dies ist ein Teils-teils-Berlin.
Aber das Komische ist,
wir haben uns ganz gut eingerichtet
in diesem Teils-teils.
In Berlin läßt sich's leben,
es ist so richtig gemütlich hier.
Aber der Schießbefehl an der Mauer?
Ich sage doch:
das Gegenteil ist immer auch wahr.
Wenn Ihnen das zu philosophisch ist,
leben Sie mal 'n Weilchen hier,
da wird Ihnen so manches ost-westlich
sehr relativ.
Auch Mauern sind relativ –
hier bei uns und in Jerusalem beispielsweise
und früher, viel früher: in China.
Naja.
Berlin, das war einmal:
keine Zeit, keine Zeit, keine Zeit.
Aber seit Goebbels im Sportpalast gröhlte:
Wollt Ihr den totalen Krieg?
Und die Bomben fielen
und Schukow kam und der Muschik
und Stalin die Blockade machte
und die Ostberliner Arbeiter den 17. Juni
und Chruschtschow das Ultimatum 58
und die Kommunisten 61
sich dieses Denkmal setzten
aus Stacheldraht und Beton…
seitdem haben wir hier gelernt,
wie angenehm das sein kann:
einmal nicht in den Schlagzeilen,
einmal historisch nicht „in",
einmal nicht „Blickpunkt Berlin".

With a Small "Well – yes"

Tell me, Berlin, what you are.
Tell it to me in your own way:
with self-deprecating irony,
a bit pert, a bit sentimental,
realistic, optimistic, dry –
with that small "Well – yes"
after every big statement.

What would you like to hear?
We can offer a whole collection
of dandy ready-made headlines:
Free City of West Berlin,
Turntable Between East and West,
City of Encounters,
Las Vegas in the Red Sea,
Show-Window of the West,
Special Political Entity,
Front-City,
Outpost of Freedom.
Don't we want, for a change,
to leave all the Berlin clichés
to one side?
Or is that itself already another cliché?
You see,
the difficulty about Berlin is:
part of everything is true,
but the opposite also is true.
If you ask me personally,
then I ask you back:
Why in fact should Berlin,
I mean West Berlin,
always have a special mission?
Of special missions we've had enough.
Now history
has pensioned us off –
as Imperial Capital to begin with,
but also as
Outpost,
Front-City,
Show-Window,
Turntable.
And when you've made
and gone through as much history
as Berlin,
then you step aside quite willingly
for others –
for those on the other side, for example,
in the Capital of the GDR.

Partly-partly –
there you have it, I think,
this whole Berlin,
which today still is only
half a Berlin –
from wherever one looks at it
This is a partly-partly Berlin.
But the funny thing is,
we've settled in quite well
in this partly part.
You really can live in Berlin,
it's genuinely gemütlich here.
And the order at the Wall to shoot?
As I say,
the opposite is also always true.
If that's too philosophic for you,
then just live a little while here,
and many an east-west matter will become
very relative for you.
Walls also are relative –
here and in Jerusalem, for example,
and earlier, much earlier: in China.
Well – yes.
Berlin, in earlier days:
No time, no time, no time.
But ever since Goebbels in the Sportpalast yelled:
"Do you want total war?"
and the bombs fell,
and Zhukov came, and the muzhik,
and Stalin ordered the Blockade,
and East Berlin's workers
staged the June 17th uprising,
and Khrushchov delivered the 1958 ultimatum,
and the Communists in 1961
built themselves this monument
out of barbed wire and concrete…
since then we've learned
how agreeable that can be:
for once not in the headlines,
for once not historically "in,"
for once not "The Focal Point Berlin."

Kurfürstendamm – Kranzlereck | The Kurfürstendamm – "Kranzler Corner"

Brandenburger Tor von Westen
Panzer vor dem Sowjetischen Ehrenmal im Tiergarten

The Brandenburg Gate from the west
the tank before the Soviet Memorial of Honor in the Tiergarten

Schloß Charlottenburg

U-Bahnhof Zoo mit „Gedächtniskirche" und Europa-Center

Charlottenburg Castle

The Zoo subway station with the Memorial Church and the Europa-Center

Olympiastadion 1936 zu den XI. Olympischen Spielen erbaut

The Olympic Stadium built 1936 for the XI. Olympics

Kongreßhalle
im Tiergarten 1957
Entwurf
Hugh Stubbins

The Congress Hall
built 1957 in the
Tiergarten
designed by
Hugh Stubbins

| Zweierlei Galerien | Two different galleries | ‚Die kleine Weltlaterne' in Kreuzberg | The "Kleine Weltlaterne" bar in Kreuzberg |

Neue
Nationalgalerie
1968
Entwurf
Mies van der Rohe

The New National
Gallery 1968,
designed by
Mies van der Rohe

| Weltberühmte Kunstwerke in Berlin | Internationally known works of art in Berlin | Nofretete 14. Jh. v. Chr. Ägyptisches Museum gegenüber dem Schloß Charlottenburg | Nofretete 14th century B.C., Egyptian Museum opposite Charlottenburg Castle |

Rembrandt
„Der Mann mit dem Goldhelm"
Gemäldegalerie im Museum Dahlem

Rembrandt
"The Man in the Golden Helmet" in the Dahlem Museum

Internationale
Grüne Woche
Messehallen am
Funkturm

International
Green Week
Exhibition halls
at the Funkturm

Der Funkturm
1924 – 1926 für
die Funkausstellung
erbaut

The Funkturm
built 1924-1926
for the Radio
Exposition

Das Renaissance-Theater, eines der etwa 20 Westberliner Theater

The Renaissance Theater, one of some 20 West Berlin theaters

Die Philharmonie 1963 Entwurf Hans Scharoun | The Philharmonie 1963 designed by Hans Scharoun

„Amüsement rund um die Uhr" – z. B. im 'New Eden Saloon' am Kurfürstendamm

"Fun around the clock" for instance in the "New Eden Saloon" on the Kurfürstendamm

Wochenend' im „Jrünen" ... | Weekend al fresco ... | ... auf dem Tegeler See | ... on Tegel Lake

... an der Krummen Lanke | ... at the Krumme Lanke

Jahrhunderte sehen dich an –	Centuries regard you –
mal gerade und monumental,	now straight and monumental,
mal schräg oder eckig und funktional.	now oblique or angular and functional.
Schinkels bescheidener Klassizismus	Schinkel's modest classicism
war schon imperial	was itself imperial
gegenüber den ärmlichen Anfängen:	compared with the pitiful beginnings:
Kölln, ein Hügel im Spreebogen,	Kölln, a hill at a bend in the Spree,
inmitten slawischer Wälder.	in the midst of Slavic woods.
Im Dreißigjährigen Krieg	During the Thirty Year's War,
kommt die Hälfte aller Berliner um.	half the Berliners died.
Wiederaufbau, nichts Neues für Berlin.	Reconstruction – nothing new for Berlin.
Hugenotten, Protestanten: Flüchtlinge –	Huguenots, Protestants: refugees –
Notaufnahme, nichts Neues für Berlin.	asylum. Nothing new for Berlin.

Deutsche Oper Berlin
1961
Entwurf
Fritz Bornemann

The Deutsche Oper
Berlin
1961 designed by
Fritz Bornemann

Acht Jahrhunderte
Bauen in Berlin

Eight Centuries
of Building in Berlin

Links: Dorfkirche
Marienfelde,
13. Jh., Romanik
Mitte: St. Nikolai
14. Jh., Gotik
Rechts: Jagdschloß
Grunewald
16. Jh., Renaissance

Left: Marienfelde
village church
13th cent., Romanesque
Centre: St. Nikolai Church
14th century, Gothic
Right: Grunewald Castle
16th cent., Renaissance

Links: Spandauer
Zitadelle mit Juliusturm
14.–16. Jh.
Mitte: Schloß
Charlottenburg
1700, Barock
Rechts: Silbersalon
Friedrichs des
Großen im Schloß
Charlottenburg
1740, Rokoko

Left: Spandau Citadel
14th–16th century
Centre: Charlotten-
burg Castle
1700, Baroque
Right: Frederick
the Great's silver
salon in the Char-
lottenburg Castle
1740, Rococo

Links: Schloß
Bellevue im Tiergarten
1785, Frühklassizismus
Mitte: Lustschloß
Pfaueninsel
um 1800, „Romantik"
Rechts: Das Humboldt-
schlößchen in Tegel
von Schinkel
1821, Klassizismus

Left: Bellevue Castle
in the Tiergarten,
1785, early Classical
Centre: The Lustschloss
on Peacock Island,
c.1800,"Romantic period"
Right: Humboldt
Castle in Tegel
by Schinkel,
1821, Classical

Links: Bürgerhaus
um 1900
(Bleibtreustraße)
Jugendstil
Mitte: Corbusierhaus
in Neuwestend
1957 (Interbau)
Rechts: Punkthoch-
haus am „Steglitzer
Kreisel", 1972

Left: Town house
c. 1900
(Bleibtreustrasse)
Art nouveau
Centre: Le Corbusier's
apartment house,
1957, (Interbau)
Right: Building
at the "Steglitzer
Kreisel" 1972

Ein verwegener Menschenschlag

Einen verwegenen Menschenschlag
mit Haaren auf den Zähnen
hat euch Berliner schon Goethe genannt.
Seid ihr verwegen? Und keß?
Herz mit Schnauze, großkotzig?
Oder seid ihr „Menschen wie du und ich"?

Kommen Sie mal ins Olympia-Stadion,
Fußball, Hertha BSC, Tor!
Oder auf 'n Heuboden im Sportpalast,
da sehen Sie die Volksseele kochen.
Oder: „Pack die Badehose ein,
nimm dein kleines Schwesterlein,
und dann nischt wie raus nach Wannsee":
Oma im lachsroten Unterrock,
Vater beim Skat, Kofferradio,
Thermosflasche, Sektorengrenze, Bikinis.
Oder stellen Sie sich vor,
was ein Museumswärter am Sonntagnachmittag
in Dahlem träumt.
Die Rentnerin in Moabit,
am Fenster, allein, hat bessere Zeiten gesehen,
schlechtere übrigens auch.
Berlinerinnen: acht Stunden an der Maschine,
strammer Pulli, fester Freund,
Blick starr auf den Feierabend gerichtet.
Oder die Frau im Kiosk:
Filzstiefel, Witwe seit Vierzig,
liebt nur noch einen: Pinscher Friederich.
Unsere Gammler sind so
wie die in Stockholm, zahmer vielleicht.
Die Blumenfrau vom Potsdamer Platz
ist umgezogen zum „i-Punkt".

Hinterhöfe im Wedding sind wie in Harlem,
nur die Kinder weiß statt schwarz.
Im Europa-Center schwingt die kleine Tina
ihr kurzes Röckchen genauso übers Eis
wie little Betsy im Rockefeller Center,
midtown New York City.
Subway, U-Bahn, Métro –
der Unterschied liegt in der Differenz.
Sonntagsreiter in schwarzer Kappe, rotem Rock,
die machen sich hübsch vorm Jagdschloß Grunewald,
aber sie sähen nicht anders aus,
ritten sie in den Bois de Boulogne,
nur daß den kein Todesstreifen
vom übrigen Frankreich trennt.
Und der berühmte Berliner Taxichauffeur?
Zwar würde er nie sagen:
„Unmögliches erledige ich sofort,
Wunder dauern etwas länger" –
aber er fährt so.
Gruppenbilder sind Glücksache:
der Taxichauffeur, die Berlinerin…
Es kommt darauf an, wen Sie treffen.
Eines vielleicht unterscheidet
uns hier tatsächlich von anderen:
Wir ha'm keen' Dialekt.
Und das verbindet uns zwei Millionen im Westen
mit der restlichen Million Berliner drüben.
Dies ist eine Stadt von Eigenbrötlern,
sie können auch Individualisten sagen.
Laubenpieper, Balkonakrobaten,
sogar die Nutten gehen nicht mit jedem,
die Selbstmordrate ist die höchste Europas,
aber schon vor 1945, ganz unpolitisch.
Verstehen Sie mich recht:
Wir sind Leute, wie die meisten Leute
in großen Städten eben sind.
Wir sind gar nicht scharf auf den Sonderstatus.
Was heißt das schon: verwegener Menschenschlag.
Heldentum, „Insulaner" – danke satt.
Blättern Sie um,
die nächste Seite kommt bestimmt
im Buch der Geschichte.
Und auf der übernächsten, in diesem Buch,
begrüßt Sie jemand,
naja, Lokalpatriotismus ist uns ja fremd –
so etwas wächst eben nur in Berlin –
taufrisch wie 'ne Weiße mit Schuß:
wohl bekomm's!

An Audacious, Plucky Breed

An audacious, plucky breed
who show plenty of fight
– that's what Goethe called you Berliners.
Are you audacious, plucky? And saucy?
"Heart-and-jaw," bigmouthed?
Or are you "People like you and me"?

Come along to the Olympic Stadium –
Soccer, Berlin's Hertha team, goal!
Or up to the top rows in the Sportpalast,
there you find the popular soul
at its boiling point.
Or, as the old song put it:
"Get your bathing-suit and Little Sister
and head out for the lake in Wannsee":
Grandma in salmon-pink slip,
Father with his Skat-cards, portable radio,
thermos bottle, american sector limits, bikinis.
Or just imagine what a Dahlem Museum attendant
dreams on a Sunday afternoon.
The old lady on a pension in Moabit,
at the window, alone, has seen better days –
and, incidentally, worse.
The girls of Berlin: eight hours at the machine,
tight sweater, steady boyfriend,
just waiting for the end of the day's shift.
Or the woman in the kiosk:
felt boots, widow since '40, with one thing
left to love: her Pinscher Friederich.
Our hippies are like those in Stockholm,
only maybe gentler.
The flower-woman from the Potsdamer Platz
has moved to the "i-Punkt" penthouse bar.

Areaways in Wedding are like those in Harlem,
except with white children instead of black.
In the Europa-Center, little Tina
flashes her tiny skirt over the ice
just like little Betsy in Rockefeller Center
in midtown New York City.
Subway, U-Bahn, Métro –
the difference lies in the dissimilarity.
Sunday riders in black caps and red jackets
pretty themselves
at the Grunewald hunting castle,
but they'd look no different
were they riding in the Bois de Boulogne,
except that no death-strips would separate them
from the rest of France.
And the famous Berlin taxi-driver?
He in fact would probably never say:
"The impossible I do immediately;
miracles take a little longer" –
but he drives that way.
Group pictures are a matter of luck:
the taxi-driver, the Berlin girl . . .
it all depends on whom you encounter.
One thing perhaps, in fact,
distinguishes us from others:
We have (it says here) no dialect.
And that binds the two million of us in the West
to the million Berliners on the other side.
This is a city of individualists –
rugged individualists, you might even say.
Nature fans, balcony acrobats –
even the whores don't go with just anybody.
The suicide rate ist Europe's highest,
but even before 1945, quite unpolitical.
Please understand me correctly:
We are simply people like
most other big-city people.
We have no real interest in our special status.
What does that really mean:
audacious, plucky breed.
Heroism, "island-dwellers" – thanks, we've had it.
Turn ahead,
the next page will definitely come
in the book of History.
And on the one after that, in that book,
there someone will greet you…
(local pride is alien to us; well – yes)
someone such as you find only in Berlin –
fresh as a Berlin Weissbier
with a shot of raspberry:
To your health!

Berliner | Berliners

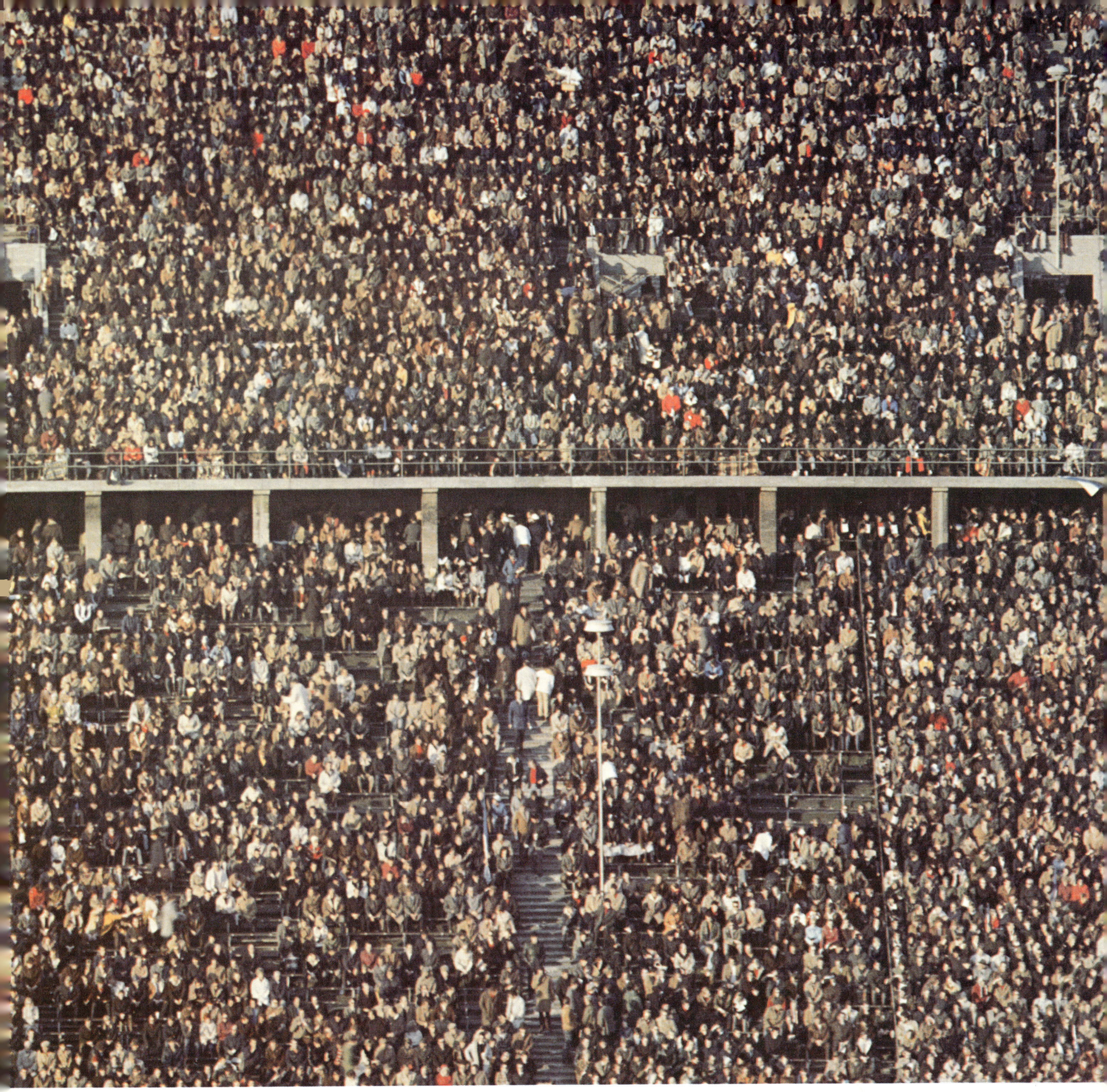

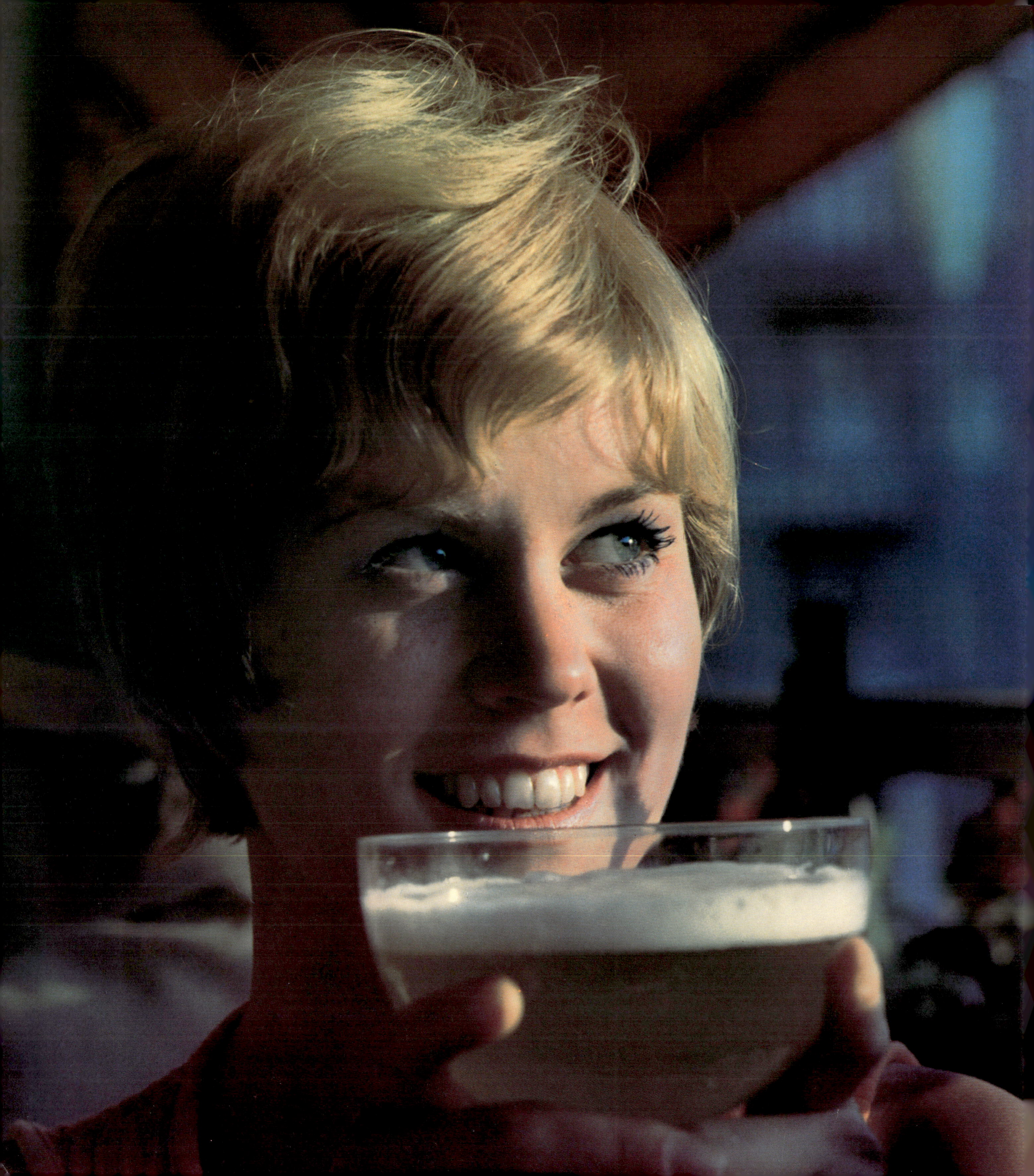

„Berliner Weiße mit Schuß"
Berlin whitebeer with a shot of syrup

Blumenfrau am „i-Punkt"
Flower-vendor at the "i-Punkt"

An der
Kaiser-Wilhelm-
Gedächtnis-
kirche

At the Kaiser Wilhelm
Memorial Church

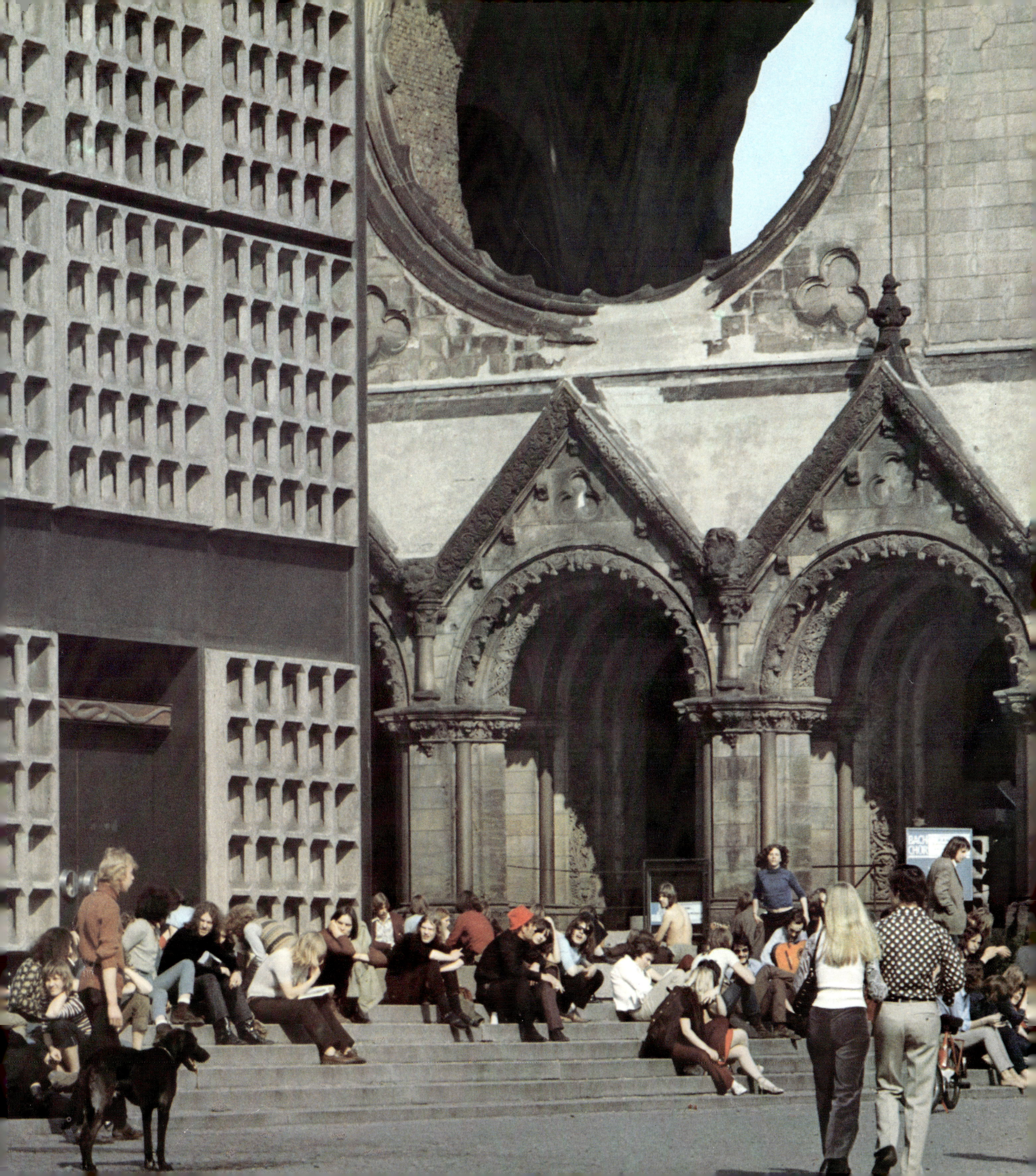
BACH

Gottesdienst
in der
Kaiser-Wilhelm-
Gedächtnis-Kirche
Neubau 1961
Entwurf
Egon Eiermann

Services
in the Kaiser Wilhelm
Memorial Church
Rebuilt 1961,
designed by
Egon Eiermann

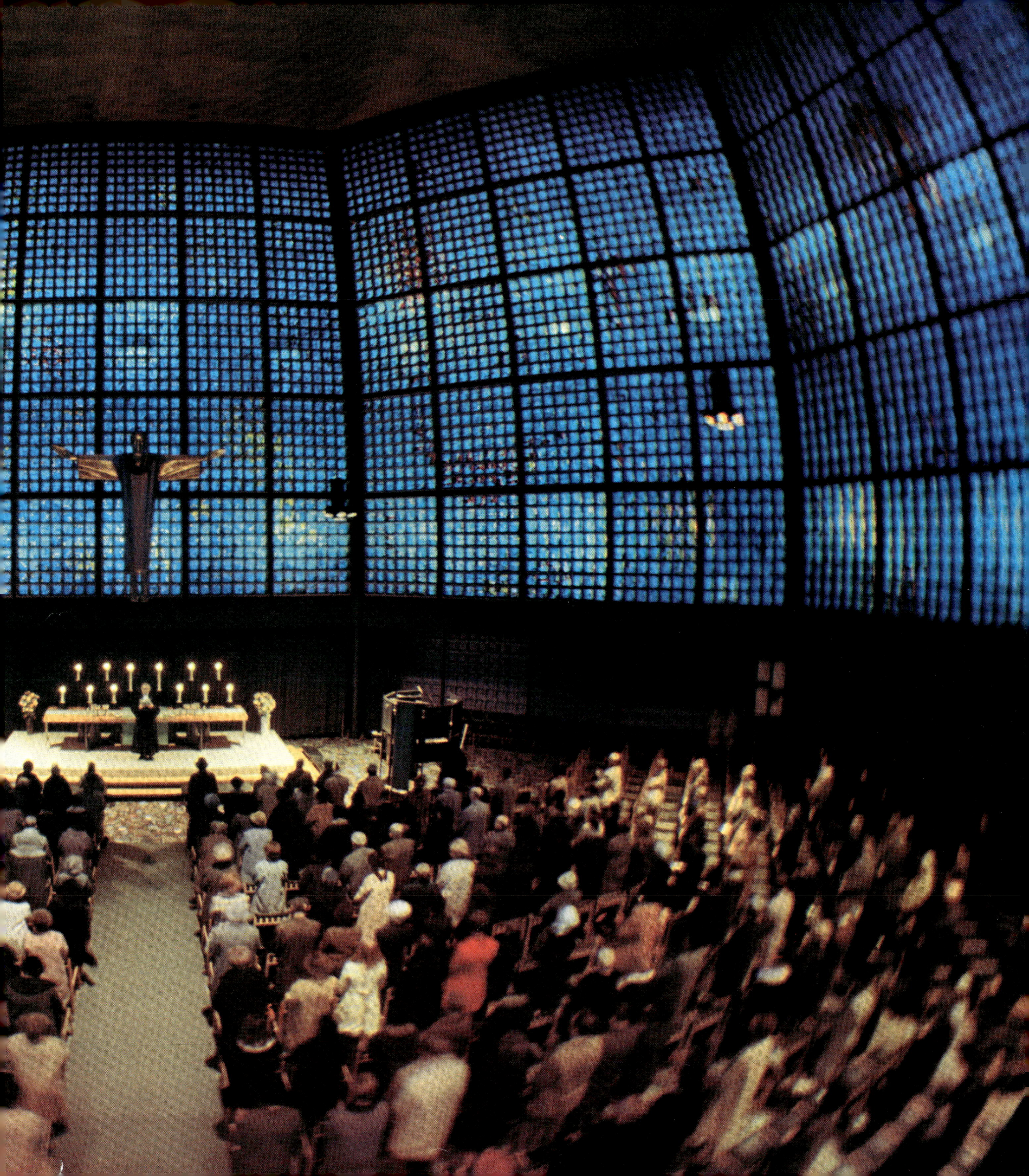

| Zeitungsfrau |
| Newspaper-vendor |

„Droschkenkutscher"
Taxi-driver

Zwei Berliner Höfe

Two Berlin courtyards

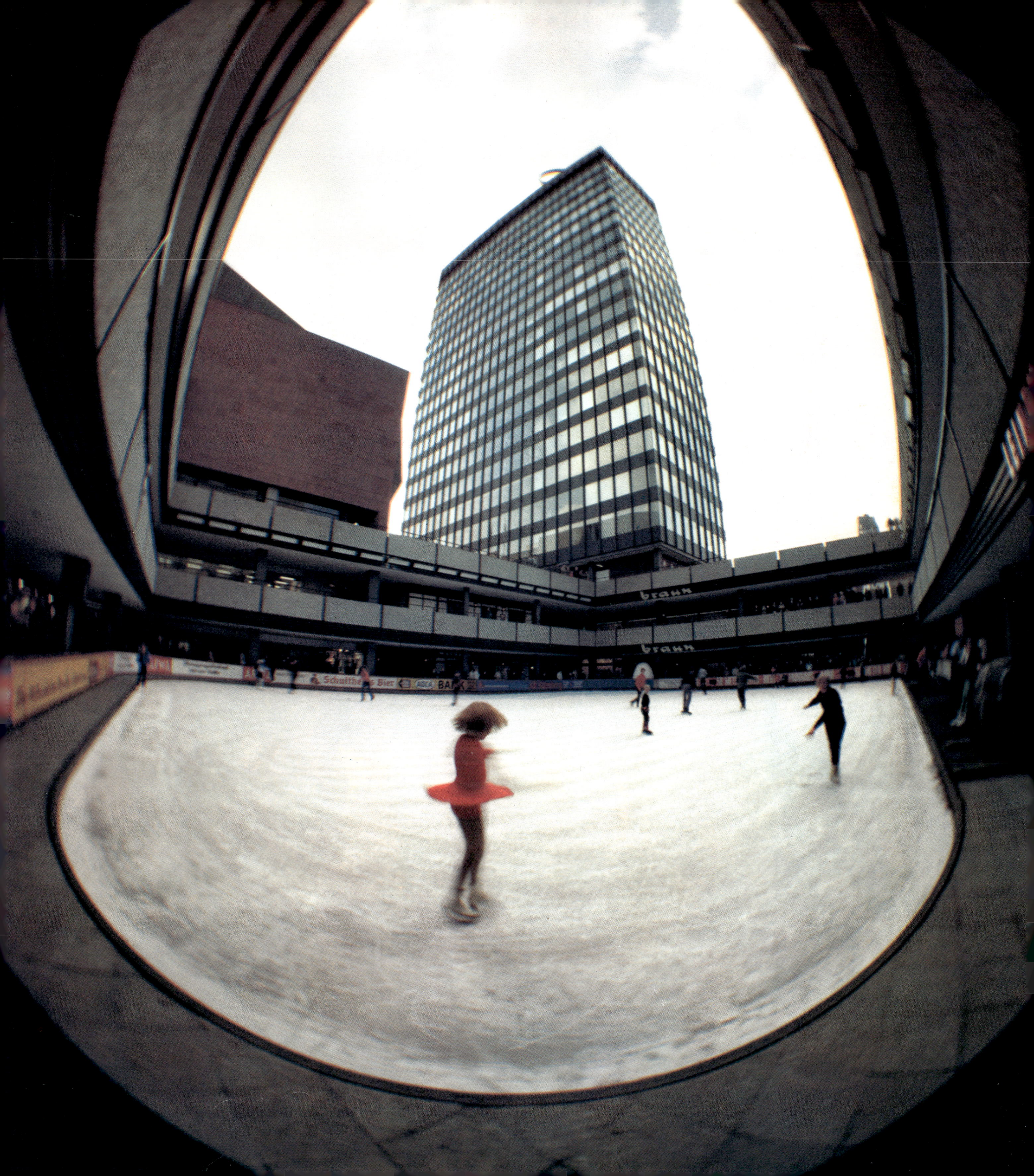

Bürohochhaus Europa-Center	Schwermaschinenbau bei Borsig
Office building in the Europa-Center	Heavy machines produced by Borsig

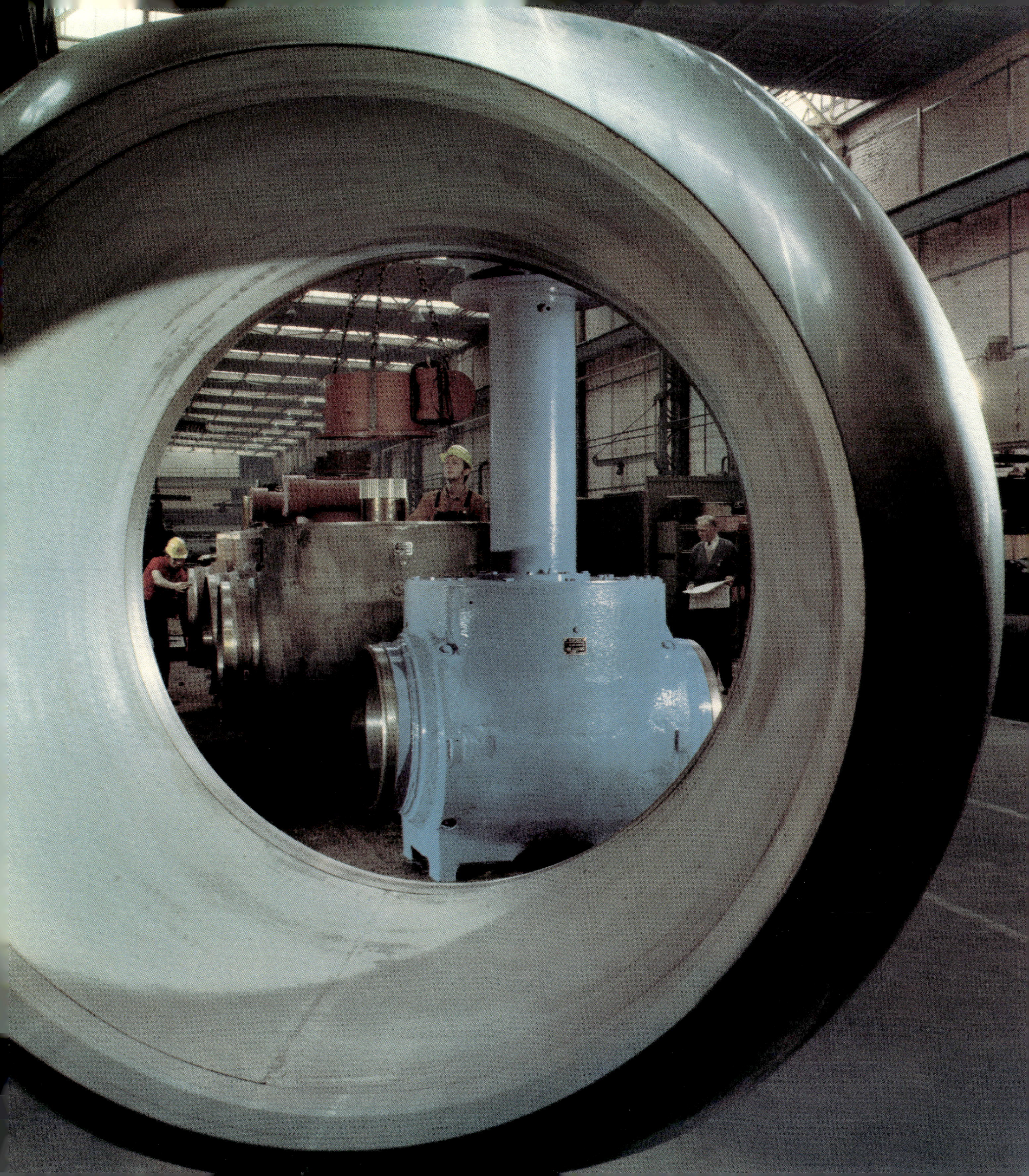

U-Bahn nach Büroschluß | Subway during rush hour

Strandbad Wannsee | Wannsee bathing beach

Unter der Hochbahn
am „Bülowbogen"
gebaut um 1900

Under the elevated
railway at the
"Bülow Curve",
built c. 1900

Gründerzeitvilla
im Grunewald

"Gründerzeit"-Villa
in the Grunewald

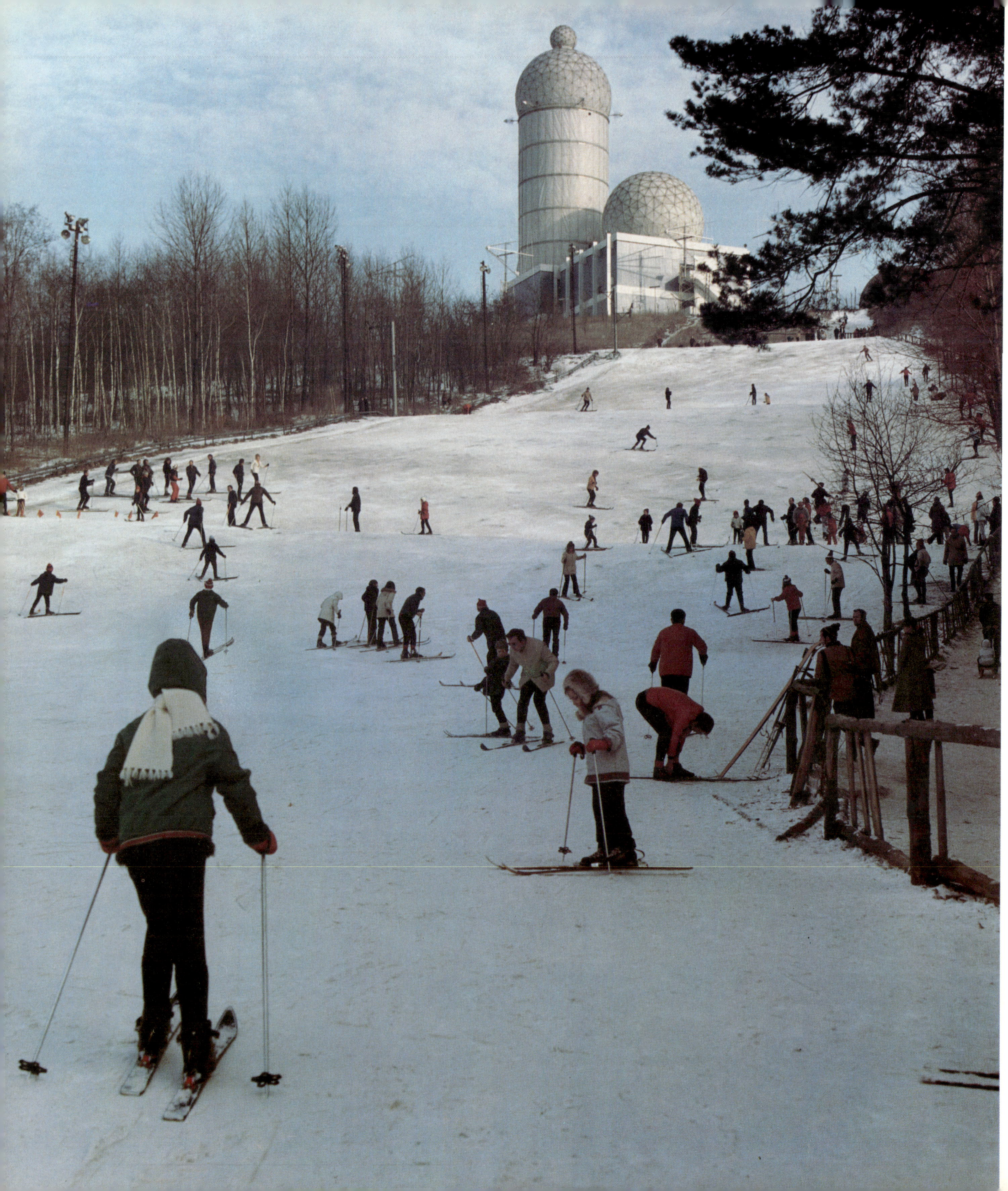

Skipiste auf dem Teufelsberg, der aus 17 Millionen Tonnen Kriegs-Trümmerschutt aufgeschüttet wurde

Ski run on Devil's Mountain, built from 17,000,000 tons of World War II rubble

„Stelldichein" zur Hubertusjagd am Jagdschloß Grunewald

Hunt rendezvous at the Grunewald Hunting Castle

Museumswärter
in Dahlem

Museum attendant
in Dahlem

Rentnerin in Moabit

Pensioner in Moabit

Zillestuben – „Heinrich heeßt'r" –
Gemüllichkeil à la Berlin.
Aber Zille, Heinrich kam aus Sachsen
und die Waldoff, Claire aus Köln.
Die gelernten Berliner liebten Berlin
oft viel inniger als die gebürtigen.
Fontane und Benn, die Hohenzollern, Liebermann.
(Und auch die drei: Windstoßer, Stuttgart;
Koch, Halle/Saale; Moor, Texas.)
Zillestuben, Nikolskoe, Aschinger, Mampe:
die Liebe zu Berlin
geht nicht nur durch den Magen – aber auch.

The Zillestuben
Gemütlichkeit à la Berlin.
But Heinrich Zille came from Saxony
and the singer Claire Waldoff from Cologne.
Adoptive Berliners have often loved Berlin
even more ardently than the native-born.
Fontane and Benn, the Hohenzollern, Liebermann.
(And also these three: Windstoßer from Stuttgart,
Koch from Halle/Saale, Moor from Texas.)
Zillestuben, Nikolskoe, Aschinger's, Mampe's:
love for Berlin
arises not only from the stomach –
but from there as well.

'Zillestuben'
Altberliner Bierlokal

The "Zillestuben"
an old Berlin
beer restaurant

Berliner Gastlichkeit

Berliner Hospitality

Links: 'Aschinger'
Mitte: 'Historischer Weinkeller' in Alt-Pichelsdorf
Rechts: 'Berliner-Weiße-Stube' im Berlin-Museum

Left: "Aschinger's"
Centre: The "Historische Weinkeller" in Old Pichelsdorf
Right: The Berliner White-beer Bar in the Berlin Museum

Links: „Strandlokal" am Tegeler See
Mitte: 'Hühner-Hugo'
Rechts: 'Blockhaus Nikolskoe' an der Havel

Left: Beach tavern at Tegel Lake
Centre: "Hühner-Hugo's" chicken grill
Right: The "Nikolskoe" Blockhouse on the Havel River

Links: Terrassen-restaurant am Kurfürstendamm
Mitte: Kaffeeklatsch bei 'Kranzler' – und überall in Berlin
Rechts: 'i-Punkt-Café', Europa-Center

Left: Restaurant terrace on the Kurfürstendamm
Centre: Kaffeeklatsch at Café "Kranzler" – and everywhere in Berlin
Right: The "i-Punkt" penthouse bar in the Europa-Center

Links: 'Mampes Gute Stube' am Ku'damm
Mitte: 'Golden-West' im Berlin-Hilton
Rechts: Grill im 'Palace-Hotel'

Left: "Mampe's Gute Stube" on the Kurfürstendamm
Centre: The "Golden West" in the Berlin Hilton
Right: The Palace Hotel Grillroom

Grazie und Gemüt

Poesie einer Großstadt,
gibt es das in Berlin?
Ist Berlin irgendwo schön?
Faszinierend war die Stadt immer –
aber schön?

Das können Sie auch von London sagen,
von Moskau, Wien und Madrid.
Anders sieht Lissabon aus, Rom, Prag, auch Paris:
da ist der Stadtkern noch immer
bestimmt von einer imperialen Idee.
Berlins alte City?
Zerbombt und außerdem: drüben,
jenseits der Mauer.
Hier bei uns, in Westberlinchen?
Naja, wir haben immerhin Charlottenburg.
Es heißt so nach Sophie Charlotte,
Kurfürstin, Königin später,
die philosophische genannt.
Sie ließ „das Lustschloß" bauen,
um Siebzehnhundert, Eosander von Göthe
später Knobelsdorff, Langhans schufen es.
Friedrich der Große wohnte hier gern,
im Park begraben „uns're" Königin –
Luise liebte dieses Schloß,
ein Zeitgenosse rühmte sie:
„Vergöttert, milde, schön und seelenvoll,
leutselig, treu, standhaft und mütterlich…"
Was, frage ich, war denn wohl so gefährlich
an diesem Schloß,
daß es zum Ziel
von alliierten Bomben werden mußte?
Dreiundvierzig: nur Schutt und Asche noch.
Die Berliner lieben ihr Charlottenburger Schloß,
wie es Sophie Charlotte und Luise liebten.
Zehn Jahre später war der Mitteltrakt
schon wieder aufgebaut,
der Park begann sich zu erholen,
das Belvedere – Friedrich Wilhelm pflog,
so sagt man, Umgang hier mit „Geistern" –
ist wieder Traumziel junger Liebespaare.

Sie sagen: schöön,
schön war Berlin noch nie,
doch faszinierend immer.
Ich finde das ganz gut.
Geht's Ihnen nicht mit Leuten ähnlich?
Ne schöne Frau, naja,
ne faszinierende, die ist mir lieber.
Wenn Sie mich aber fragen,
worin die Attraktivität Berlins besteht?
Ich will es Ihnen sagen:
vielleicht gerade im teils teils.
Berlin dynamisch, gut.
Berlin erstaunlich tolerant, naja.
Berliner Volksmund witzig, stimmt.
Berlin mit beiden Beinen auf der Erde, ja.
Berlinerinnen knusprig, realistisch, liberal –
Berliner quick, freiweg und ohne Falsch –
klingt alles freundlich und: naja.
Und nehmen Sie dazu das gute Wetter,
die Luft, von der der alte Bismarck sagt:
wie Sekt –
dann haben Sie die Mischung,
und die macht's.
Großstadt und Poesie?
Das gibt's
nicht nur im Park Charlottenburg
und auf Watteaus „Cythère",
das finden Sie in jeder Toreinfahrt
im letzten Kietz,
kommt nur drauf an,
mit wem Sie drunter schmusen.
Erotisch ist Berlin,
sagt mancher, der hierher verschneit,
so mit uns eine Weile lebt.
Das hören wir ganz gern – wer nicht.
Gemüt und Grazie,
Liebe zu den kleinen Dingen,
heiteres Darüberstehn,
das kann durchaus auch preußisch sein,
Sie finden's bei Fontane,
Sie finden's in den Winkeln
dieser großen Stadt –
und freilich niemals auf den ersten Blick.
Ein Nicht-Berliner hat den Nagel
mal wieder auf den Kopf getroffen,
aus Dresden kam er und heißt Kästner,
Berlin – das war ihm:
„Herz auf Taille".

Grace and Feeling

The poetry of a great city,
does it exist in Berlin?
Is Berlin anywhere beautiful?
Fascinating the city always was –
but beautiful?

You can say the same about London,
about Moscow, Vienna and Madrid.
Lisbon looks different, Rome and Prague, too,
also Paris: there an imperial idea
still dominates the heart of the city.
The heart of old Berlin?
Bombed out; and, in addition, over yonder,
beyond the Wall.
Here on our side, in our little West Berlin?
Well – yes. After all, we still have Charlottenburg.
It's named that for Sophie Charlotte,
Princess, later Queen,
called "the philosophical".
She ordered this castle, the "Lustschloss", built;
about 1700, Eosander von Göthe,
later Knobelsdorff and Langhans created it.
Frederick the Great enjoyed living here;
buried in its park, "our" Queen –
Luise loved this castle
a contemporary praised her as
"adored, gentle, beautiful and soulful,
kind, loyal, stanch, and motherly…"
What, I ask you, was so dangerous
about this castle
that it had to become the target
of Allied bombs?
1943: still only rubble and ashes.
The Berliners love their Charlottenburg Castle,
just as Sophie Charlotte and Luise loved it.
Ten years later the middle part
had already been rebuilt;
the park began to recover;
the Belvedere (Friedrich Wilhelm,
so they say, cultivated converse with "spirits" here)
is again the goal of dreaming young lovers.

They say: beautiful,
beautiful Berlin never was,
but fascinating, always.
I find that quite good.
Don't you find it similar with people?
A beautiful woman; well – yes;
but a fascinating one I prefer.
But if you ask me:
Where does Berlin's attractiveness lie?
Then I'll tell you:
Perhaps in its very partly-partliness.
Dynamic Berlin, good.
Astoundingly tolerant Berlin, well – yes.
Berlin's witty vox populi, right.
Berlin with both feet on the ground, yes.
Berlin's women, crisp, realistic, liberal –
Berliners alert, direct, and without phoniness –
it all sounds friendly and… well – yes.
And then add to that the good weather,
the air, of which old Bismarck said:
like champagne –
there you have the mixture,
and that's what counts.
Metropolis plus poetry?
That exists
not only in Charlottenburg Park
and in Watteau's "Cythère":
that you can find in every gateway
in even the most remote area,
it all depends on
whom you're nuzzling there.
Berlin is erotic –
so say many whose way has led them here
and who spend a while among us.
We enjoy hearing it, who wouldn't?
Feeling and grace,
love for the little things,
cheerful aloofness –
that, too, can be entirely Prussian.
You find it in Fontane's writings,
you find it in the nooks and crannies
of this great city –
and of course never at first glance.
Once again a non-Berliner
hit the nail on the head;
he came from Dresden, name of Erich Kästner,
and for him Berlin meant
"heart made to measure".

Schloß Charlottenburg
Parkseite

Charlottenburg Castle
the park side

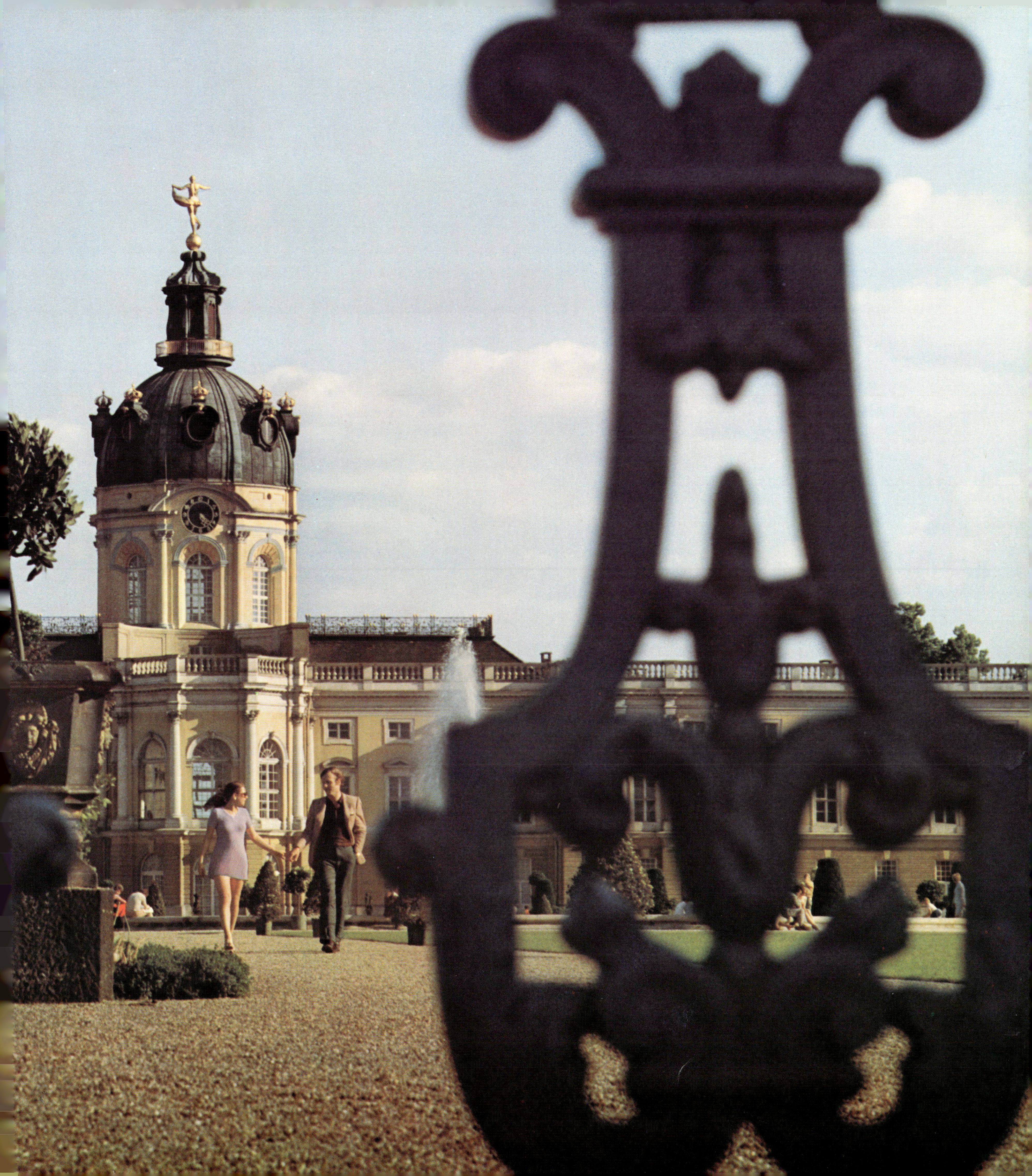

„Einschiffung zur Liebesinsel Cythera" von Antoine Watteau 1717, Gemäldesammlung Friedrichs des Großen Charlottenburger Schloß

"Embarcation for the Romantic Island of Cythera" by Antoine Watteau 1717, art collection of Frederick the Great Charlottenburg Castle

Goldener Arbeitssalon Friedrichs des Großen Charlottenburger Schloß

Frederick the Great's golden workroom Charlottenburg Castle

Amor im Spätherbst | Amor in the autumn

Amor im Frühling | Amor in the spring

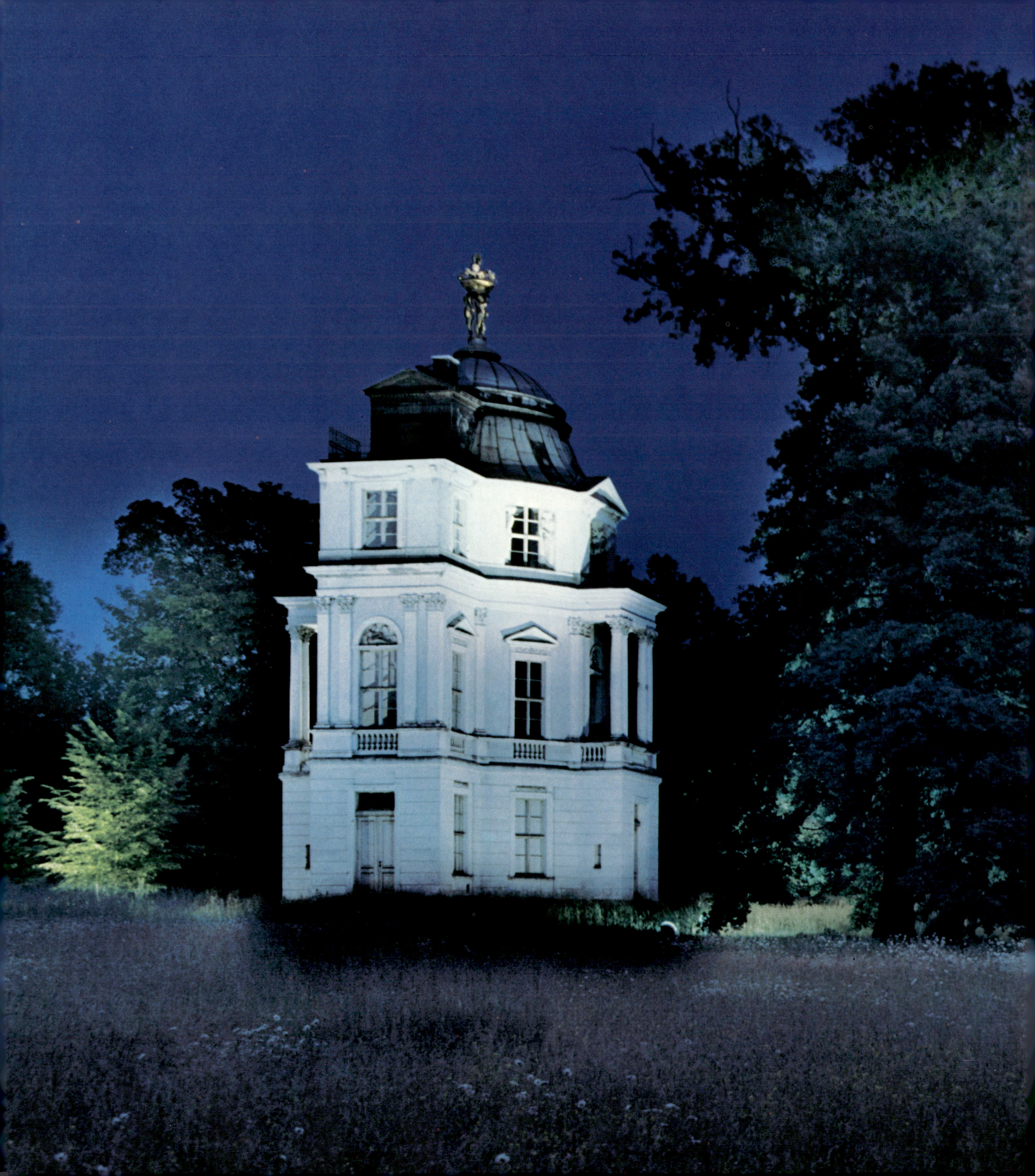

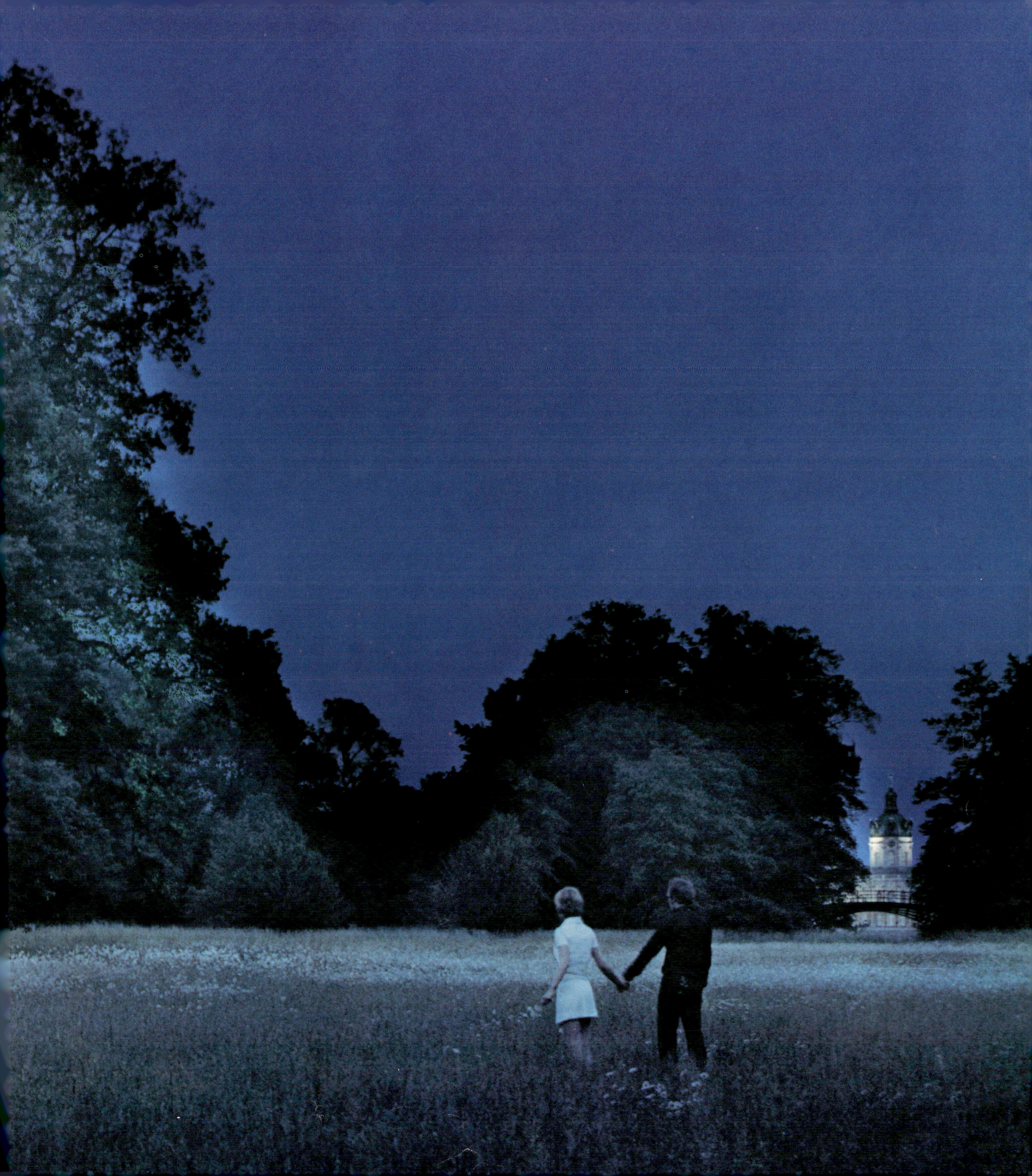

Berliner Liebespaare | Berlin lovers

1744
gemalt vom Schloß-
baumeister
Knobelsdorff

1744
painted by
the castle architect
Knobelsdorff

1972

Die Goldene
Spiegelgalerie
Charlottenburger
Schloß
1740 – 44
für Friedrich
den Großen
erbaut von
Georg Wenzeslaus
von Knobelsdorff

The Golden Gallery
of Mirrors
Charlottenburg Castle
built 1740-44 for
Frederick the Great
by Georg Wenzeslaus
von Knobelsdorff

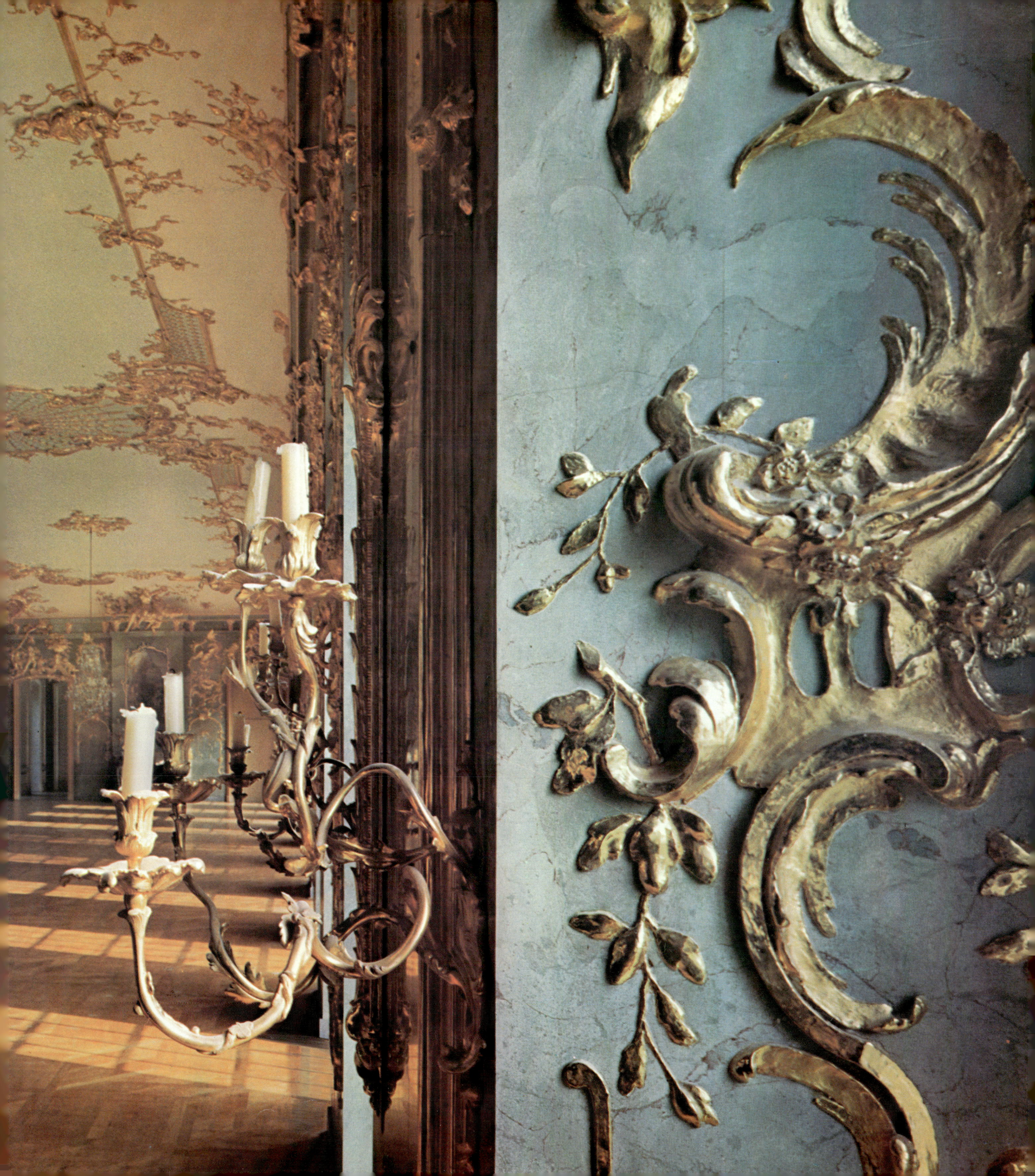

Schloßpark Charlottenburg | Charlottenburg Castle gardens

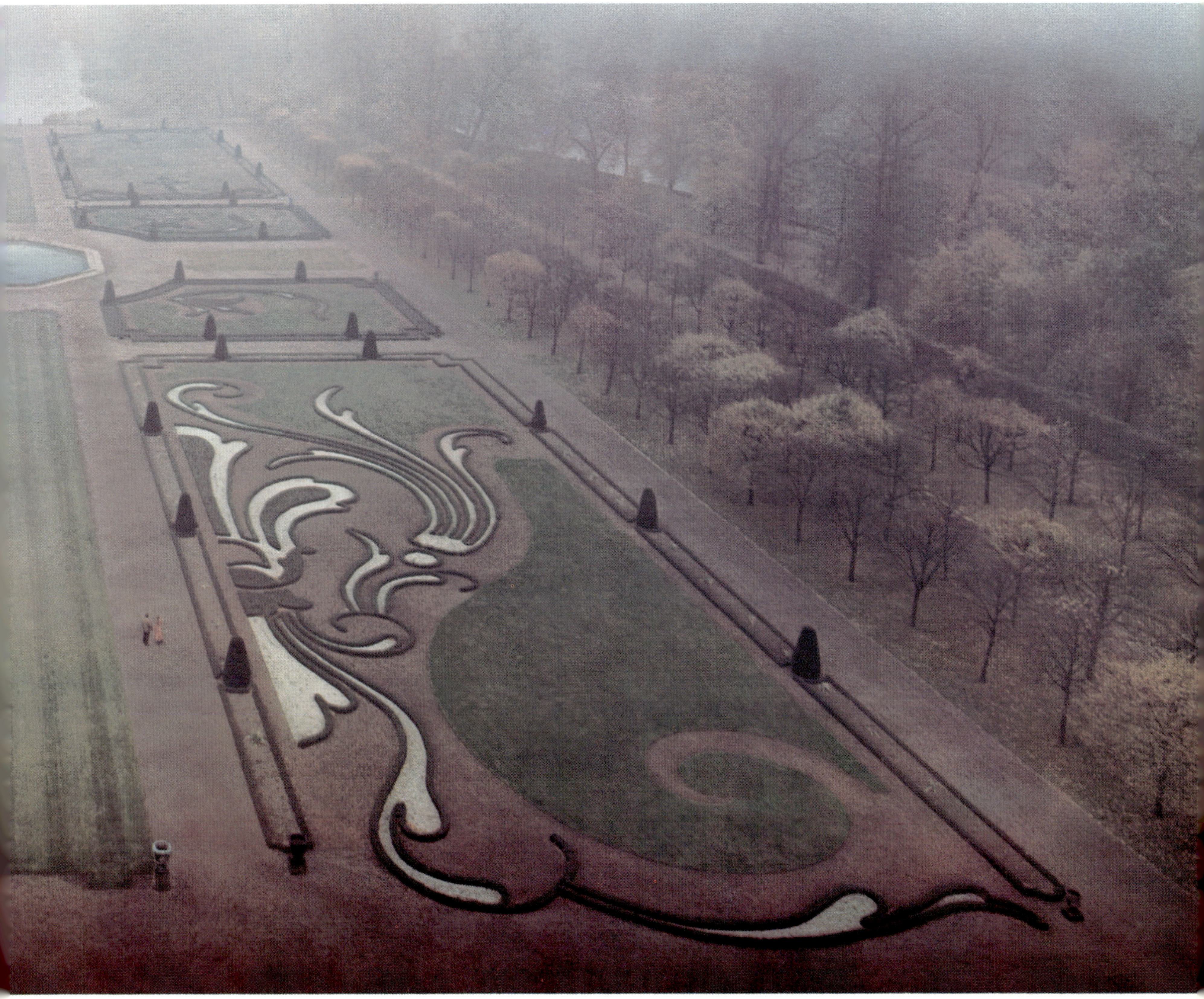

Der große Kurfürst Friedrich Wilhelm
gilt als der Gründer Brandenburgs und Preußens.
Andreas Schlüter schuf sein Denkmal,
Johann Jacobi goß es
1700 und aus einem Stück.
Zweihundertfünfzig Jahre prangte
das Reiterstandbild auf der Langen Brücke,
versank im Tegeler See nach 45.
Wurde gehoben
und beherrscht nun die Auffahrt
zum Schloß Charlottenburg:
ein Brocken preußischen Barocks.

The great Kurfürst Friedrich Wilhelm one regards
as founder of Brandenburg and Prussia.
Andreas Schlüter sculpted his monument,
Johann Jacobi cast it
in 1700 and in one piece.
Two hundred years his equestrian statue
adorned the Long Bridge,
only to sink into Lake Tegel after 1945.
Raised,
today it dominates the approach
to Charlottenburg Castle:
a monument of Prussian baroque.

Reiterdenkmal des
Großen Kurfürsten
1698 von
Andreas Schlüter

Equestrian statue
of the Great Kurfürst
1698
by Andreas Schlüter

Berlinerinnen

Berlin girls

In Porzellan
Rokoko um 1770

In porcelain, Rococo
c. 1770

Gemalt
von Antoine Pesne
um 1750

Painted
by Antoine Pesne
c. 1750

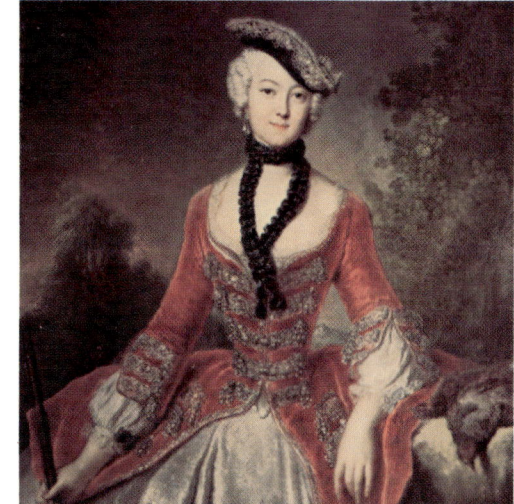

In Stein, Hermen
im Schloßpark
Charlottenburg
klassizistisch

In stone,
hermae in the
Charlottenburg Castle
gardens,
Classical

Lebend 1972

Live 1972

Das komische Dorf

Sind das nicht eigentlich mehrere Städte:
Berlin?
Nicht nur West oder Ost –
sondern auch innerhalb West-Berlins:
Avus zum Grunewald hinaus,
Tauentzien/Ku'damm,
Schrebergärten und Stadtautobahn,
Gründerzeitvillen und Märkisches Viertel,
Havel samt Wannsee, Tegeler Forst,
Achse Ost–West,
Heerstraße übers „Knie" bis zum Tor.
Sind das nicht lauter Kontraste –
und Berlin gibt nur den Namen dafür?

Naja, Sie können auch sagen: Zoo –
aber der besteht doch aus Bären
und Affen und Löwen und Zebras,
Giraffen, Kamelen und Wärtern.
Apropos Zoo,
die Gegend war früher bloß „W",
Berlin-W, bißchen feiner und stiller
als die Innenstadt: Alex, Potsdamer Platz,
Friedrichstraße und Leipziger,
heute alles drüben, jenseits.
Heute ist aus dem westlichen, kleineren Brennpunkt
der einstmals kompletten Ellipse
ein neues Zentrum geworden:
Zellteilung sozusagen im Großen.
Zwischen Nollendorfplatz und Halensee
spielt sich nun alles ab –
jedenfalls für Touristen.
Natürlich ist Berlin „ne Reise wert",
und der Bauboom sucht seinesgleichen:
Steuererleichterung lockt,
wozu sind wir kapitalistisch.
Mancher Versicherungspalast, manches Bürohaus
kratzt an der falschen Stelle
unseren preußisch-blauen Himmel.
Oft haben Baulust und Pietät
faule Kompromisse geschlossen.

Nichts gegen Wilhelm
als Kaiser und Vornamen
und als Gedächtniskirche auch meinetwegen.
Aber der hohle Zahn des Turms
und Eiermanns Blaue Grotte daneben,
soll ich da lachen oder weinen.
Der Betonbaukasten ringsum
macht mich auch nicht fröhlicher.
Vor einem grauen Hochhausraster
die kleine Anhalterbahnhof-Ruine,
das rührt mich mehr.
Früher kamen hier die Züge
aus Sachsen an und aus Schlesien.
Deutschland hat keinen Bahnhof mehr.
Hier fällt uns das manchmal noch auf,
keiner spricht mehr darüber,
die Jungen sagen auch hier:
was kümmert denn uns der Schnee
vom vorletzten Jahr. Oder:
die Schuhe sind uns zu groß.
Naja, also lassen wir das,
waren es eben nur
75 Jahre Reichshauptstadt
und danach schon wieder 25 Jahre
dieses dauerhaften Provisoriums…
teils teils.
Was in ein Jahrhundert so alles hineingeht?
Sogar ein „Tausendjähriges Reich",
das uns genau dahin brachte,
wo wir hier immer noch krebsen
und bis auf weiteres – eben teils teils.
Das wahre Berlin, Westberlin,
wo sein Herz wohl schlägt?
Krumme Lanke oder Wedding,
Roseneck, Tempelhof, Reichstag?
Ich will Ihnen ein Geheimnis anvertrauen –
aber nicht gleich sagen: wie sentimental.
Da drin in der Brust,
da ist das wahre Berlin.
Für den älteren Menschen hier
kommen die Züge noch an
am Anhalterbahnhof,
die Mauer ist bloß ein Alptraum.
Für die Jüngeren – je nachdem:
manche wollen alles anders,
die meisten sagen: naja.
Aber alle lieben das komische Dorf,
irgendwie.
Verstehen Sie das vielleicht?

This Funny Town

Isn't that actually more than just one city:
Berlin?
Not only just West or East,
but also within West Berlin:
the Avus highway out to the Grunewald woods,
Tauentzienstrasse and Kurfürstendamm,
garden colonies and the city throughway,
ancient villas and new developments,
the River Havel and its lake, Wannsee,
Tegel Forest, the East-West Axis boulevard,
the Heerstrasse past "the Knee"
to Brandenburg Gate.
Are those not merely a list of contrasts
to which Berlin only gives a name?

Well – yes; you can also say: the Zoo –
but that's comprised of bears
and apes and lions and zebras,
giraffes, camels, and attendants.
Speaking of the Zoo,
this area used to be simply "W." –
Berlin-W., a bit finer and quieter
than the city's heart: Alexanderplatz,
Potsdamer Platz, Friedrichstrasse
and Leipziger Strasse,
today all over yonder, on the other side.
Today, out of the little western focal-point
of the once complete ellipse,
has arisen a new center: division of cells,
so to speak, on a grander scale.
Between Nollendorfplatz and Halensee,
everything takes place –
at least for the tourists.
Naturally Berlin is worth a trip,
and the building boom has no equal:
tax advantages entice,
why else are we capitalistic?
Many an insurance palace, many an office building
scrapes our Prussian-blue sky
at the wrong spot.
Sense of tradition and the rage to build
have often reached queer compromises.

Nothing against Wilhelm
as Kaiser or as first name
or even, as far as I'm concerned,
as Memorial Church.
But the hollow tooth of the tower
and Eiermann's Blue Grotto next to it –
am I supposed to laugh or cry?
The concrete building block around it
doesn't make me any more cheerful.
In front of the grey background
screen of a skyscraper,
the little ruin of the Anhalter Station,
that touches me more.
The trains used to come here
from Saxony and Silesia.
Germany has no railroad station any more.
Here, sometimes, we still notice that,
nobody talks about it anymore,
here too the young say:
What's that to us, the snows
of yesteryear? Or:
Their shoes are too big for us.
Well – yes; let it go –
it was for only
75 years the Imperial Capital
and after that 25 years
of this enduring provisionality…
partly-partly.
How much you can fit into one century!
Even a "Thousand-Year Reich",
which brought us to exactly that point
where we still have a hard time of it
and until further notice –
as I said, partly-partly.
The true Berlin, West Berlin,
where does its heart really beat?
Krumme Lanke or Wedding,
Roseneck, Tempelhof, Reichstag?
I should like to confide a secret to you –
but don't say at once: how sentimental.
There in the breast,
there is the true Berlin.
For the older people here
the trains still arrive
at the Anhalter Station,
the Wall is only a nightmare.
For the younger ones – it all depends:
some of them want everything different,
most of them say: well – yes.
But all of them love this funny town,
somehow.
Do you know what I mean?

Ruine des
Anhalter Bahnhofs
vor dem Hochhaus am
Askanischen Platz

Ruins of
the Anhalter Station
before the office
building at the
Askanischer Platz

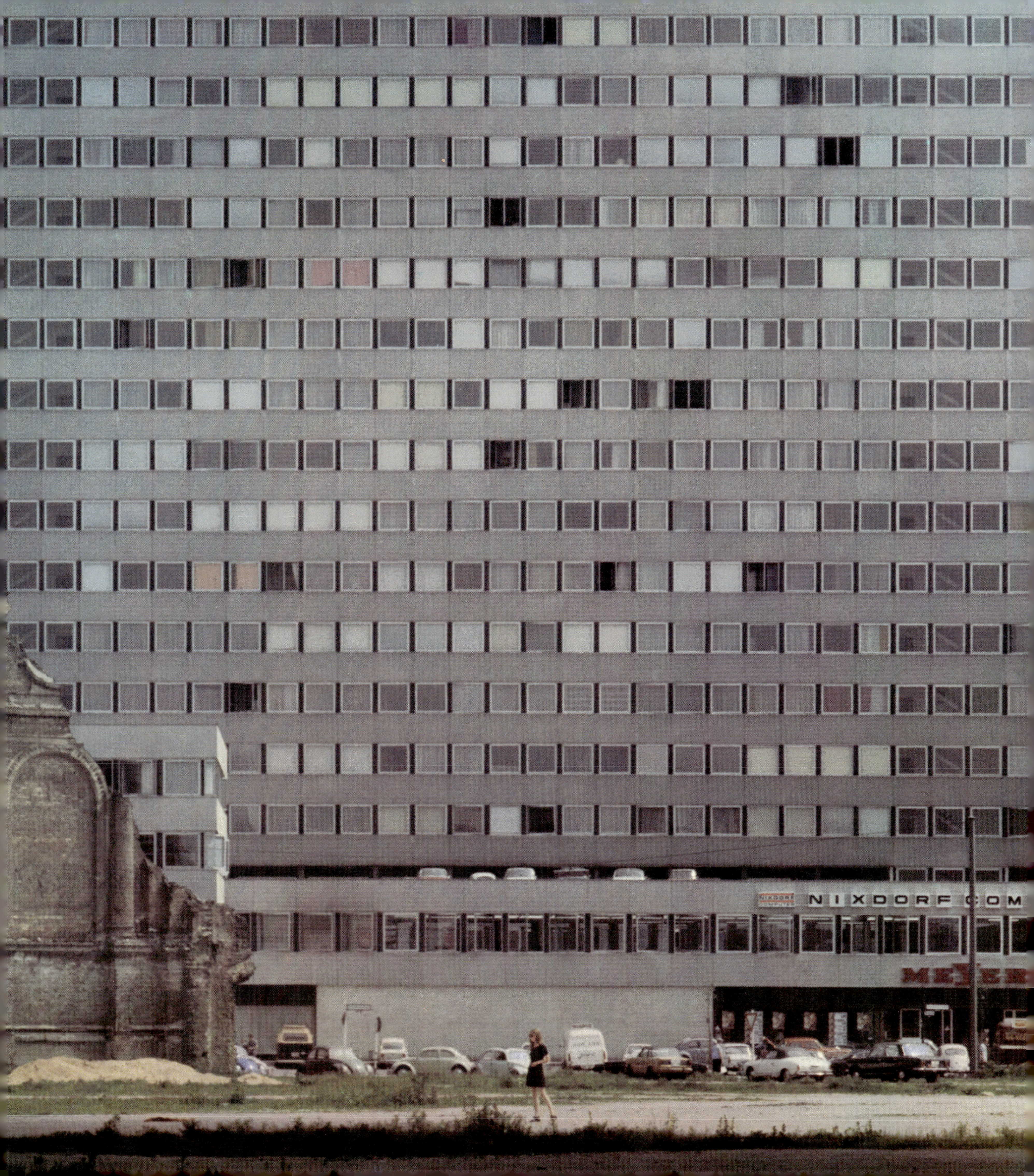
NIXDORF COM

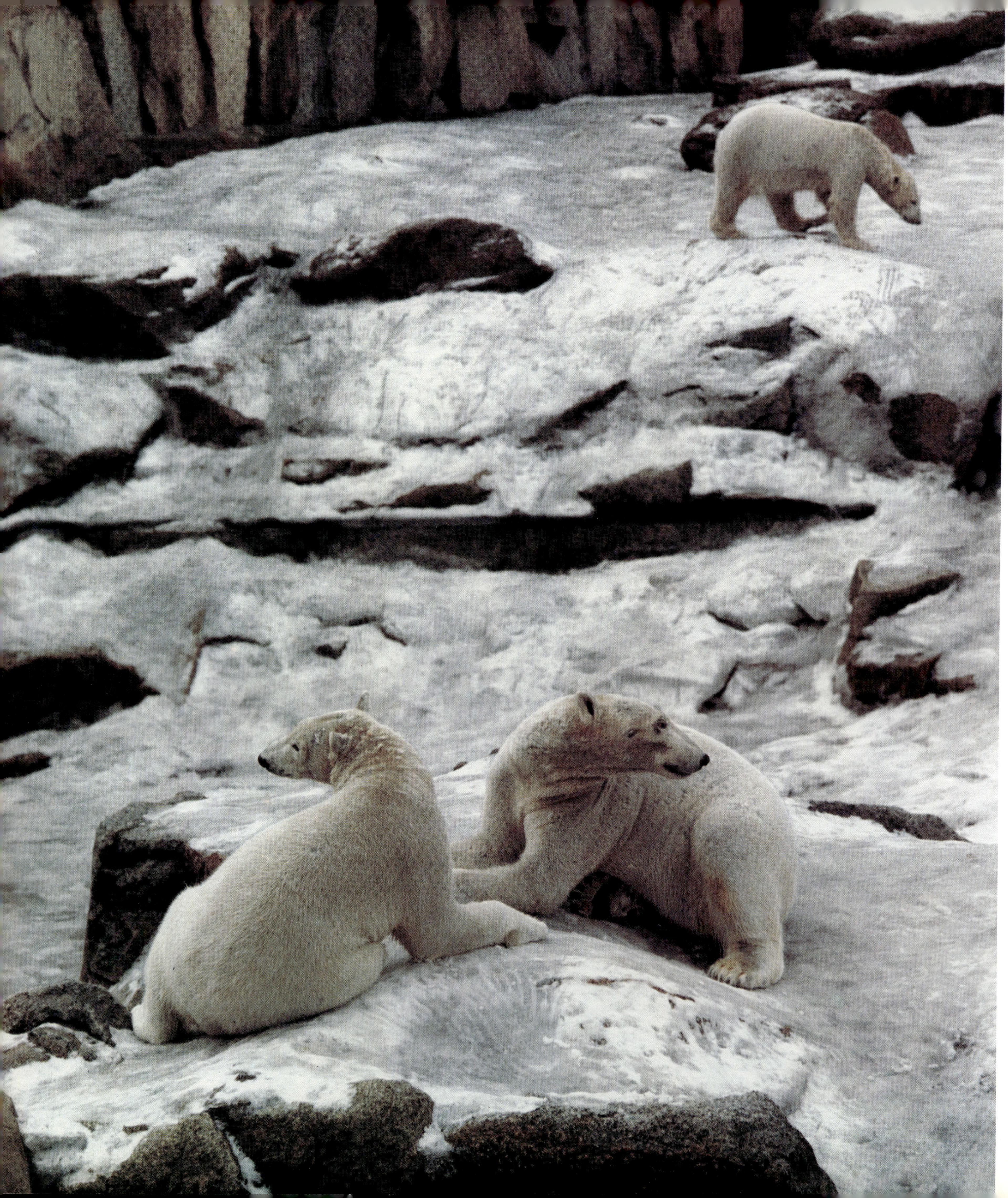

Arktis und Tropen –
Wand an Wand:

Artic and tropic –
side by side:

Eisbären im Zoo

Polar bears
in the Zoo

Krokodile im Aquarium

crocodiles
in the Aquarium

Avusrennen

Racing on the Avus speedway

Sechs-Tage-Rennen im Berliner Sportpalast

Six-day bicycle races in the Sportpalast

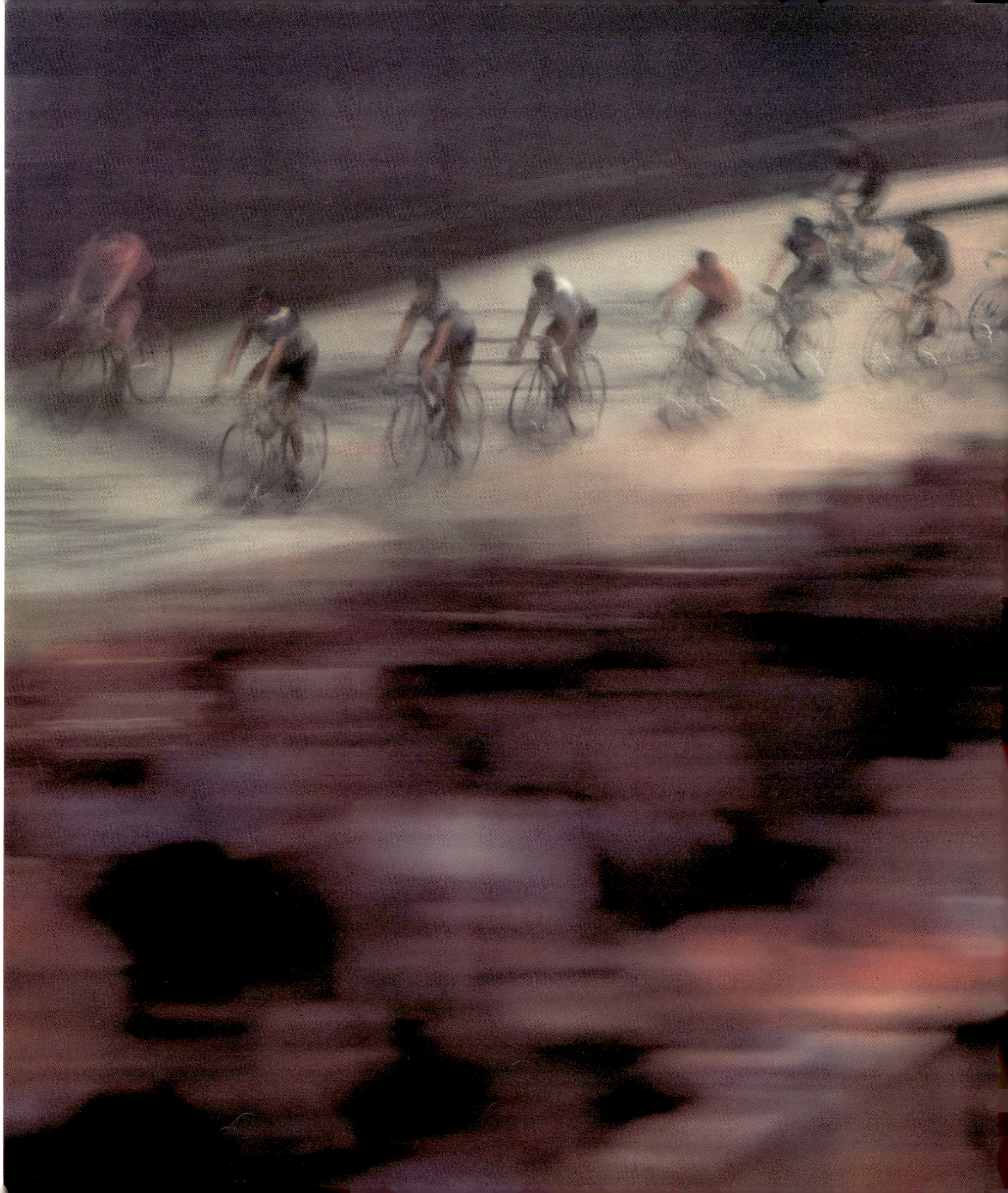

An der Mauer

At the Wall

Bernauer Straße

Verlagshochhaus an der Kochstraße, dem ehemaligen Berliner Zeitungsviertel

Newspaper building in the Kochstrasse, in Berlin's former newspaper publishing section

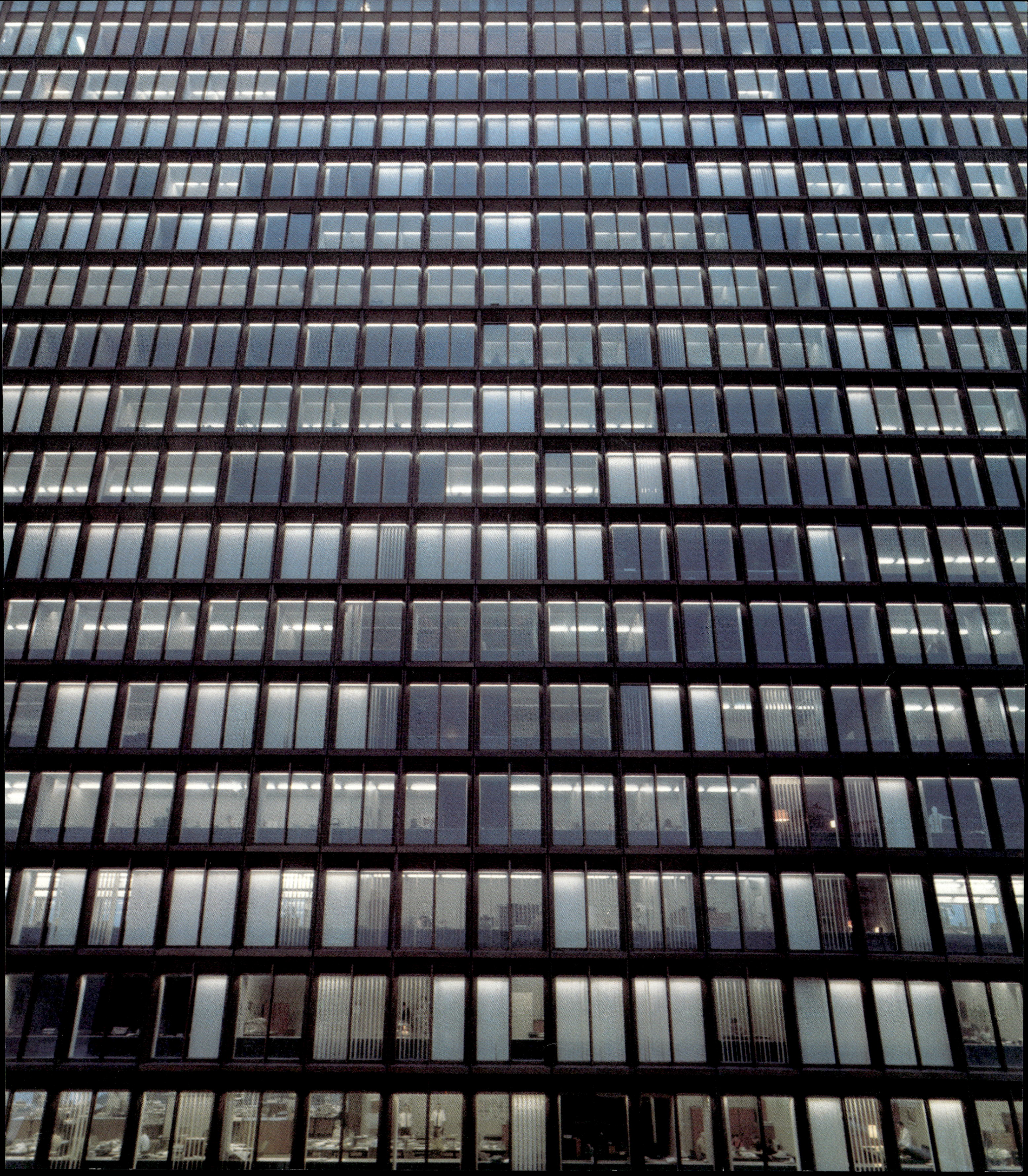

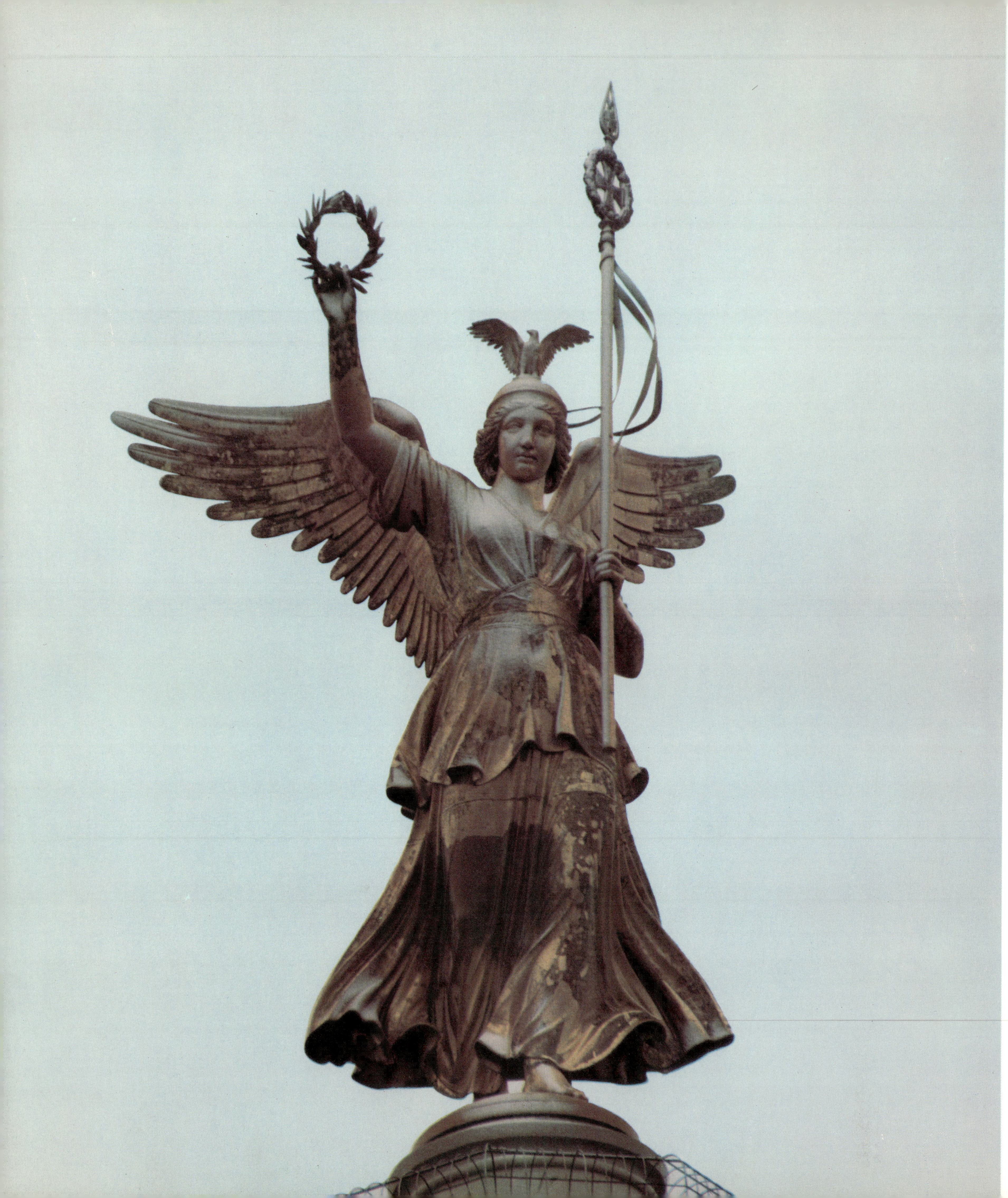

Die Viktoria
die „Gold-Else"
auf der Siegessäule
am Großen Stern

Victoria
atop the
Victory Column
in the Grosser Stern
traffic circle

Seraphische
Metallplastik von
Hans Uhlmann
vor der Deutschen
Oper Berlin

Seraphic Metal Sculpture
by Hans Uhlmann
before the
Deutsche Oper Berlin

„Der Tauentzien"
um 11 Uhr
vormittags

"Der Tauentzien"
Tauentzienstrasse
at 11 a.m.

„Der Ku'damm"
um 11 Uhr
nachts

"Der Ku'damm"
Kurfürstendamm
at 11 p.m.

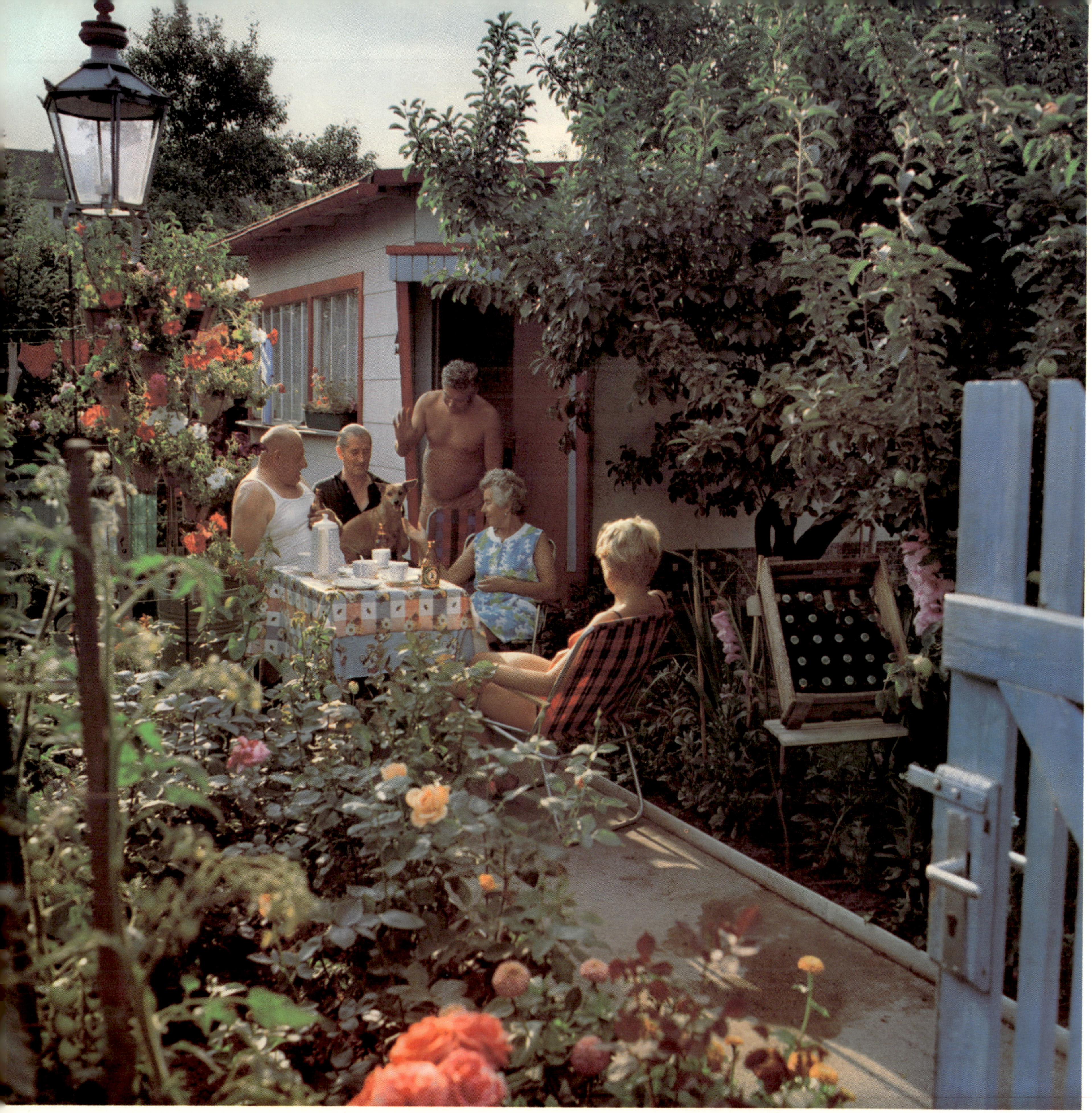

„Laubenpieper" in der
Schrebergarten-
kolonie „Roseneck"

Nature lovers
in the Roseneck
garden colony

Berliner
Biedermeier-„Milljöh"

Berlin Biedermeier
milieu

Wohnen... ...1970
Märkisches Viertel

...1890
in Kreuzberg

Housing... ...1970
Märkisches Viertel
development

...1890
Kreuzberg

Blick
vom Grunewaldturm
auf Havel
und Havelberge

View
from the Grunewald
Tower
of the Havel River
and Hills

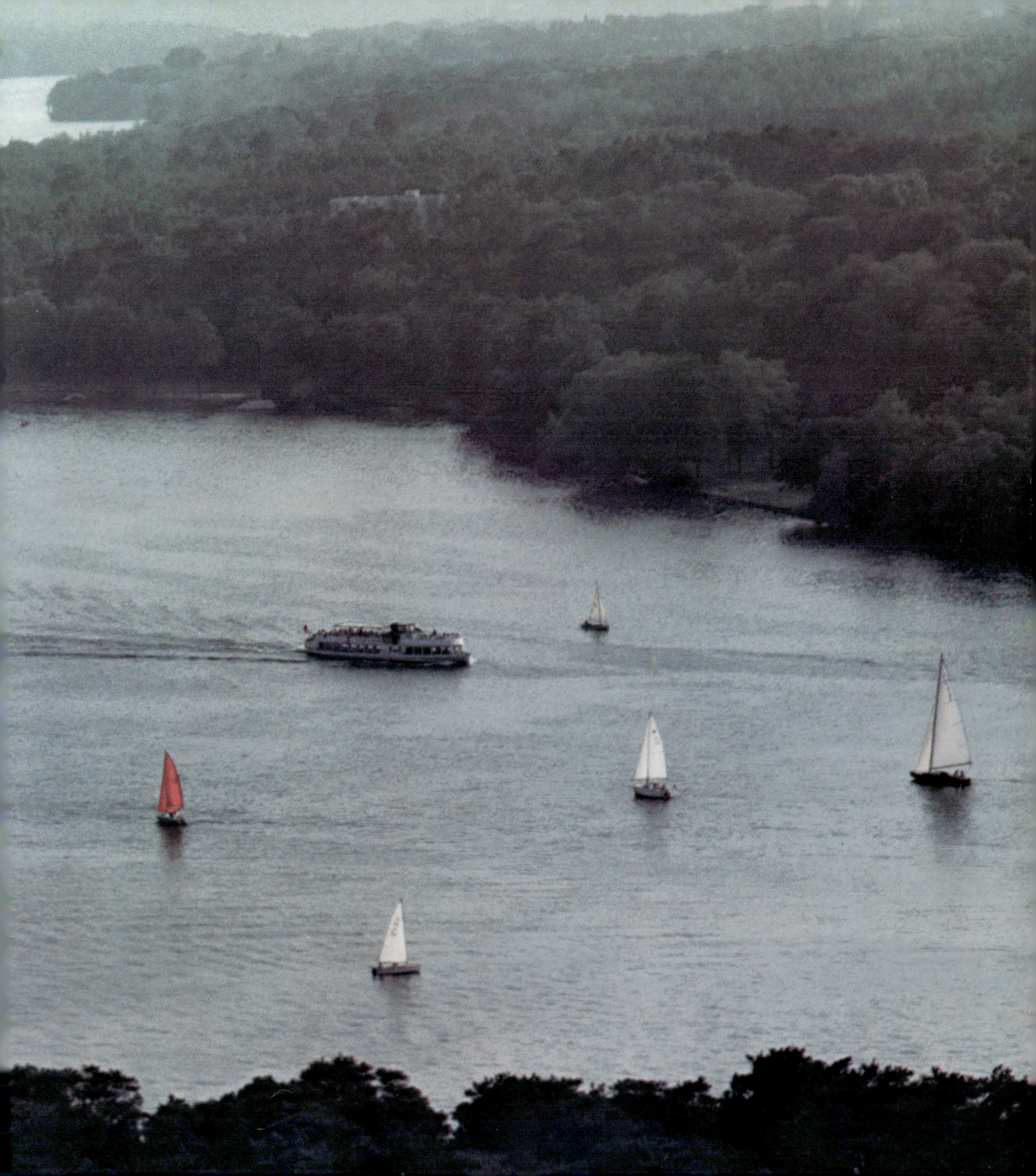

Mit mehreren PS... ...im Tegeler Forst

Horsepower... ...in Tegel Forest

... am Avus-Stadt-
autobahnverteiler

... on the
Avus cloverleaf

Kunsthandel:

Art dealers:

Der „Zillemarkt"
in der
Bleibtreustraße

The "Zille Market"
in the
Bleibtreustrasse

Die Galerie
Ben Wargin
im Europa-Center

The Ben Wargin
Gallery in
the Europa-Center

"Charleston-Eva"
der 20er Jahre
bei einem
Kreuzberger Trödler

"Charleston-Eva"
of the 1920s
at a second-hand
shop in Kreuzberg

"Eva"
von Botticelli
um 1500
im Dahlemer Museum

"Eve" by Botticelli
c. 1500,
Dahlem Museum

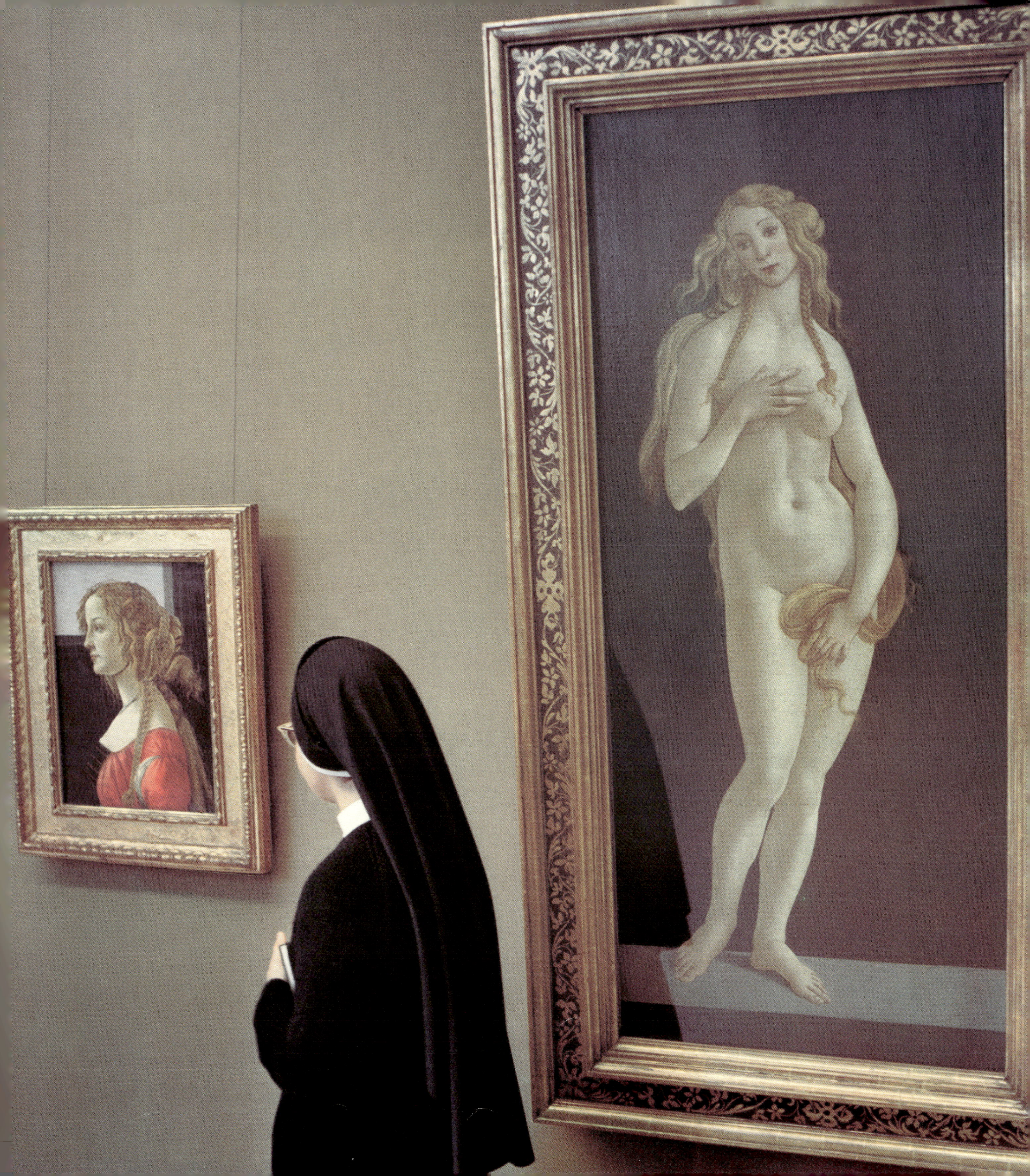

Wer Berlin 1945 sah, wird schwer begreifen, woher die Kunstwerke kommen, die heute wieder da sind: wie noch einmal geboren. Schien nicht alles verbrannt, verschüttet, zerfetzt – unwiederbringlich? Tatsächlich blieb nur ein Rest von den Schätzen vieler Jahrhunderte. Neues kam schnell hinzu, und so ist die Stadt sogar eine Kunstreise wert.	Anyone who saw Berlin in 1945 will hardly understand where the art works came from that are here again today. Did not everything seem destroyed by fire, buried in rubble, ripped to shreds – beyond recall or repair? Only a fraction did in fact remain of the treasures of many centuries. New ones came in addition, and so today the city once again merits an artistic pilgrimage.

Frühgotische Madonna um 1300 vor „Apokalyptischer Vision" Altarwand von Georg Meistermann 1963

Early Gothic Madonna c. 1300, before "Apocalyptic Vision" altar screen by Georg Meistermann 1963

Denkmäler, Skulpturen, Gemälde

Links: Aussichtshalle in Kleinglienicke von Schinkel, 1835
Mitte: Siegessäule im Tiergarten: 1870/71!
Rechts: Luftbrückendenkmal Tempelhof: Berlin-Blockade 1948/49

Left: Panorama-hall in Kleinglienicke by Schinkel, 1835
Centre: Victory Column Tiergarten: 1870/71!
Right: Airlift memorial: Berlin Blockade 1948/49

Links: Karyatide an einem Berliner Wohnhaus, Jugendstil
Mitte: Plastiken von Georg Kolbe im ehemaligen Atelier
Rechts: „Die Liegende" von Henri Laurens 1948, Nationalgalerie

Left: Art nouveau caryatid on a Berlin house
Centre: Sculptures by Georg Kolbe in his former studio
Right: "Reclining Figure" by Henri Laurens 1948 National Gallery

Links: Porträt der Königin Luise um 1800 im Schloß Grunewald
Mitte: „Flötenkonzert Friedrichs des Großen" von Adolph von Menzel, 1852, Neue Nationalgalerie
Rechts: „Fischerboot" von Max Pechstein 1913 im Brücke-Museum

Left: Portrait of Queen Luise c. 1800 in the Grunewald Castle
Centre: "Frederick the Great's Flute Concerto" by Adolph v. Menzel 1852 New National Gallery
Right: "Fishing Boat" by Max Pechstein 1913, Brücke Museum

Links: Mondrian und Monroe-Mund in der Akademie der Künste, Hansaviertel
Mitte: 'Die Spitze' Karikaturistenkneipe
Rechts: Bildermarkt um Ku'damm und Gedächtniskirche

Left: Mondrian and Marilyn's Mouth in the Academy of the Arts Hansa Quarter
Centre: "Die Spitze" caricaturists' bar
Right: Picture market, Kurfürstendamm and Memorial Church

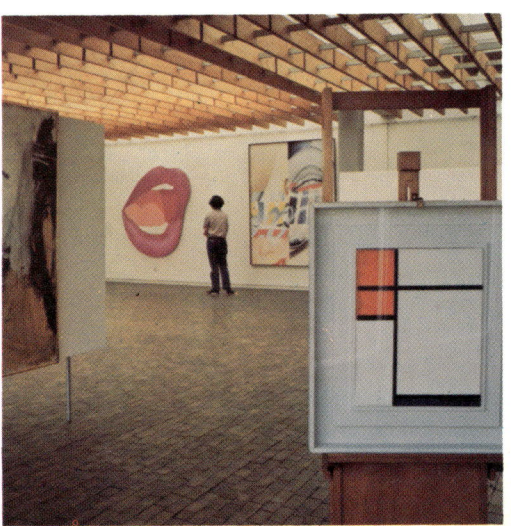

Im übrigen: man lebt

Stimmt es, daß Westberlin
im Jahr Güter und Dienstleistungen
im Wert von 25 Milliarden DM produziert?
Also kein Faß ohne Boden mehr?
Und die großen Firmen wandern nicht ab?
Was ist wahr:
überalterte Rentnerstadt,
Stadt der roten Studenten
oder fleißiges, tüchtiges,
ganz normal tätiges Westberlin?

Naja, wahr ist von allem etwas.
Und – wie ich wiederholen möchte –
das Gegenteil auch.
Wir haben viele Alte,
aber zugleich die radikalsten Jungen.
Große Firmen verlagerten
Konzernspitzen nach München und Hamburg,
sogar unser Regierender Willy
wanderte ab nach Bonn.
Aber die Antibabypille von Schering,
Stahl von Borsig,
Sendeanlagen von Siemens,
Telefunkenempfänger, AEG-Aggregate,
das alles läuft wie in der Bundesrepublik,
dieselbe Lohn- und Preisspirale.
Sogar ein Gastarbeiterproblem
nennt Westberlin jetzt sein eigen –
Vollbeschäftigung und mehr als das.
Rudi Dutschke wurde
am Kurfürstendamm angeschossen,
die linke Kritik überlebte,
stellt das westliche System in Frage,
verhöhnt „immanente Kritik",
funktioniert um, was die Väter
an Freiheit retteten und im Kalten Krieg
gegen die Kommunisten etablierten.
Ernst Reuter wäre für die Roten Zellen
an der Freien und an der Technischen Uni
nichts als ein „scheißliberaler Opa".
Kann „das System" die jungen
Marx-Entdecker und Mao-Schreihälse verkraften?
Es präsentiert sich nicht stets überzeugend,
dieses System.
Viel ist verkrustet:
in den Parteien, bei Presse und Funk.
Zeitungen dürfen hetzen,
NS-Richter weiter und wieder richten,
Ohnesorg-Töter Kurras wird freigesprochen,
qualifizierte Professoren kapitulieren,
Reformmodelle pervertieren.

Gutes Theater noch auf den Bühnen,
schlechtes zuweilen im Alltagsparkett.
Mancher zieht sich zurück –
ins Atelier,
in seine Kneipe,
ins ganz Private –
und fliegt so oft wie möglich
von Tempelhof oder von Tegel
nach Gran Canaria oder Tunesien,
denn gut verdienen,
das kann man durchaus in Berlin.
Warenhaus, Fachgeschäft, stille Boutique –
Berliner Chic verkauft sich gut,
hier am Ort, für'n Export:
was da mit Nadel und Schere
Couturiers und Nähmädchen leisten,
schlägt sich oft besser im Auftragsbuch nieder
als so manches klotzige Triebwerk
oder Großforschungsgerät.
Und außerdem:
Ernst ist das Leben,
heiter aber meistens ist Mode,
wenn sie nicht gerade,
aufgehängt an busenlosen Mannequins,
entschlossen scheint,
die Frau zur Männerscheuche zu machen.
Und das woll'n wir nicht in Berlin.
Fazit: die Wahrheit über Westberlin?
Wir sind nicht „in", nicht „out",
die „Subventionsmentalität"
beflügelt Arbeitsproduktivität.
„Eliten-Exodus" und so
verursacht geistige Provinzialität?
Mag sein, doch wo
ist heute intellektuell Saison?
Im übrigen: man lebt.

And, by the Way: One Lives

Is it true that West Berlin
annually produces goods and services
of about $ 8,000,000,000 in value?
No longer, then, a "barrel without a bottom"?
And the great firms do not leave?
Which is true:
overage city of pensioners,
city of red students,
or industrious, able,
quite normally active West Berlin?

Well – yes; part of all that is true.
And, as I'd like to repeat, the opposite as well.
We have many old people,
but at the same time the most radical youth.
Great firms transferred
their headquarters to Munich and Hamburg,
even our mayor Willy Brandt
wandered off to Bonn.
But "the pill" from Schering,
steel from Borsig,
transmitters from Siemens,
Telefunken receivers, AEG installations –
all just the same as in the Federal Republic,
with the same spiralling wages and prices.
Today West Berlin can even call
a "problem" with foreign workers its own –
full employment and even more.
Rudi Dutschke, the leftist student,
was shot and wounded on the Kurfürstendamm,
but leftist criticism survived,
questioning the western system,
mocking "immanent criticism",
changing what the fathers
rescued in the way of freedom
and during the Cold War
established against the Communists.
Divided Berlin's western mayor Ernst Reuter,
for the Red Cells
at the Free and the Technical Universities,
would today be nothing but
a "lousy liberal grandpa".
Can "the system" assimilate the young
Marx-discoverers and Mao-bawlers?
It presents itself as not always convincing,
this system.

Much is barnacled over:
in the parties, the press, the other media.
Newpapers may incite,
Nazi judges may judge further or once again,
a student-killing policeman wins acquittal,
qualified professors capitulate,
reform plans become perverted.
Good theater on the city's stages,
bad now and then in the streets of everyday.
Some withdraw –
into the studio,
into the bar,
into the completely private sphere –
and fly as often as possible
from Tempelhof or from Tegel
to Grand Canary or Tunesia,
for making good money
presents no problem in Berlin.
Department store, specialty shop, quiet boutique –
Berlin chic goes over well,
here at the source as well as for export:
what couturiers and seamstresses accomplish
with needle and scissors
counts for more in the order-book
than many a massive power-plant
or giant scientific machine.
And in addition:
Life is serious,
but fashion is mostly cheerful,
except for such times as when,
hung upon bosomless mannequins,
it seems determined
to turn women into frights.
And that we don't want in Berlin.
The sum total: the truth about West Berlin?
We are not "in", not "out",
the "subsidy mentality"
lends wings to working productivity.
An "exodus of the elite" and so on
gives rise to provincialism of the spirit?
Could be; but where today
will you find intellectual high season?
In addition: one lives.

Siemensstadt: | Siemens City:
30000 Beschäftigte | 30,000 employees

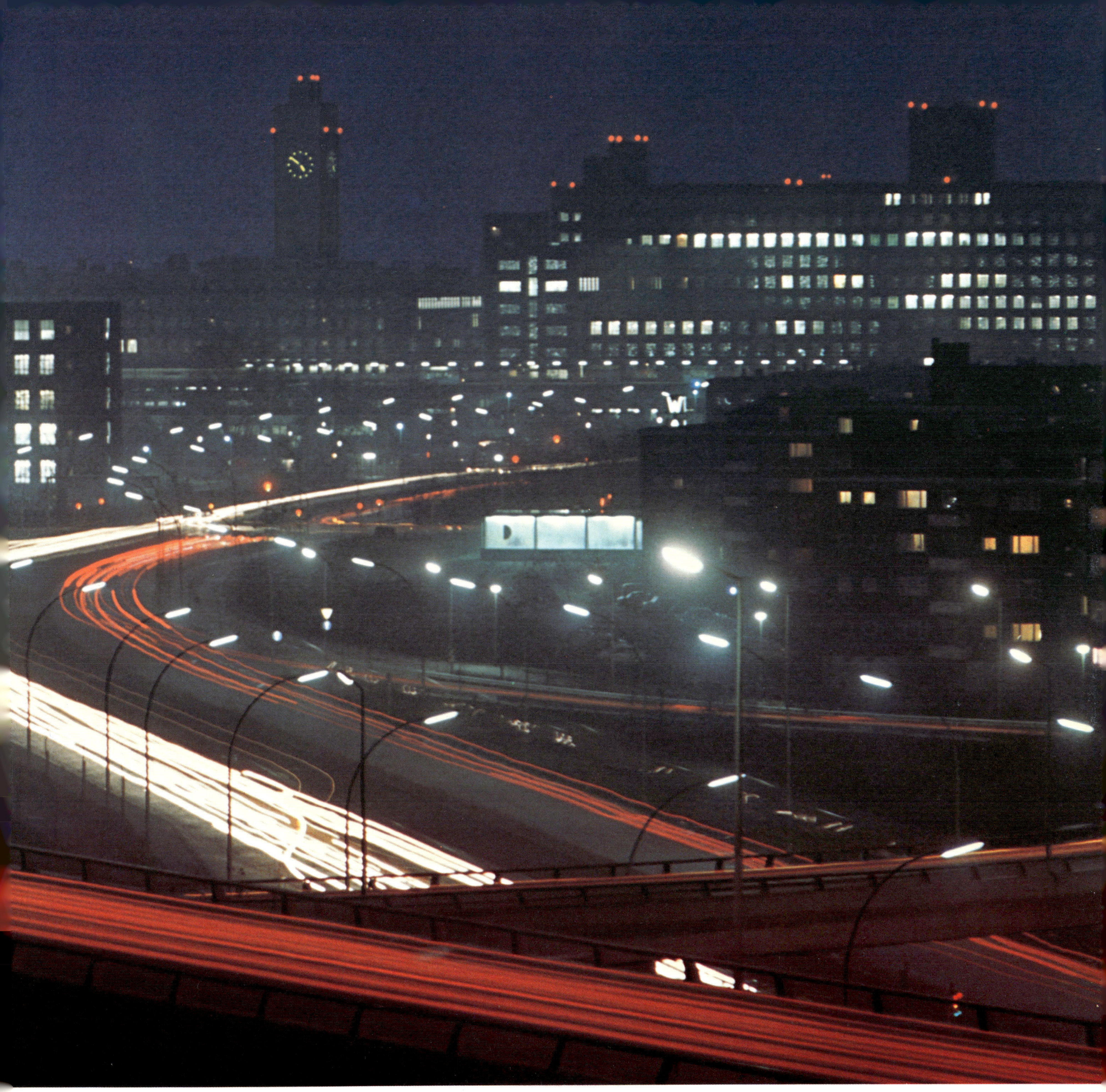

AEG-Großmaschinenhalle | AEG's heavy machinery plant

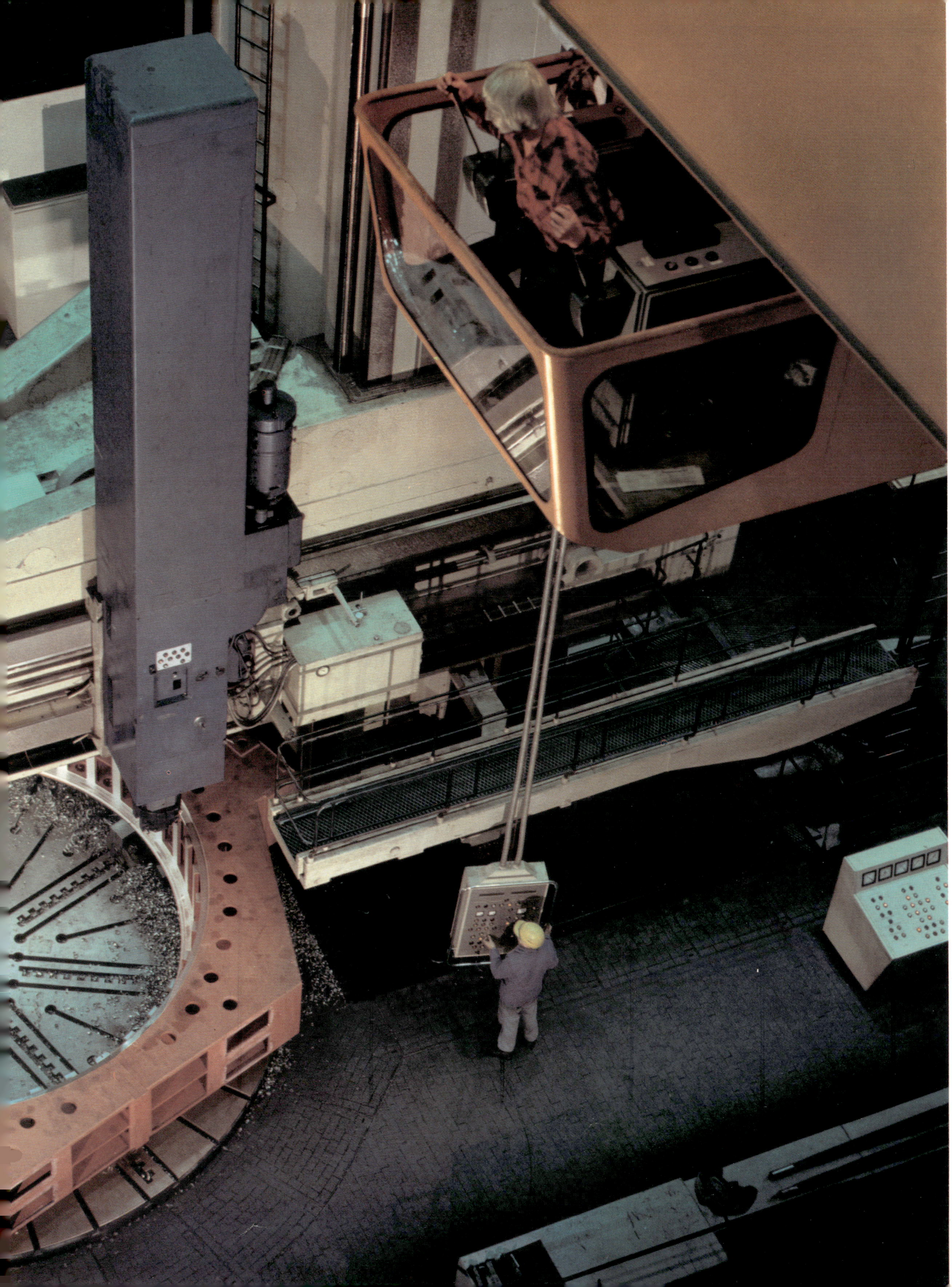

„Berliner Chic":
"Berliner chic"

im Atelier...
in the atelier...

... auf dem Laufsteg
bei der
„Durchreise"

... on the runway
during the annual
"Durchreise" show

KaDeWe
NOCH
größer
IM SOMMER SCHLUSS VERKAUF
KaDeWe
NOCH
größer
IM SOMMER SCHLUSS VERKAUF
RESTE
Restposten
Donnerstag
Freitag
Sonnabend

„Ka De We"
Kaufhaus des
Westens
am Wittenbergplatz

"Ka De We"
department store
on the Wittenbergplatz

Montage
eines Elektromotors
bei Siemens

Assembling
an electric motor,
Siemens works

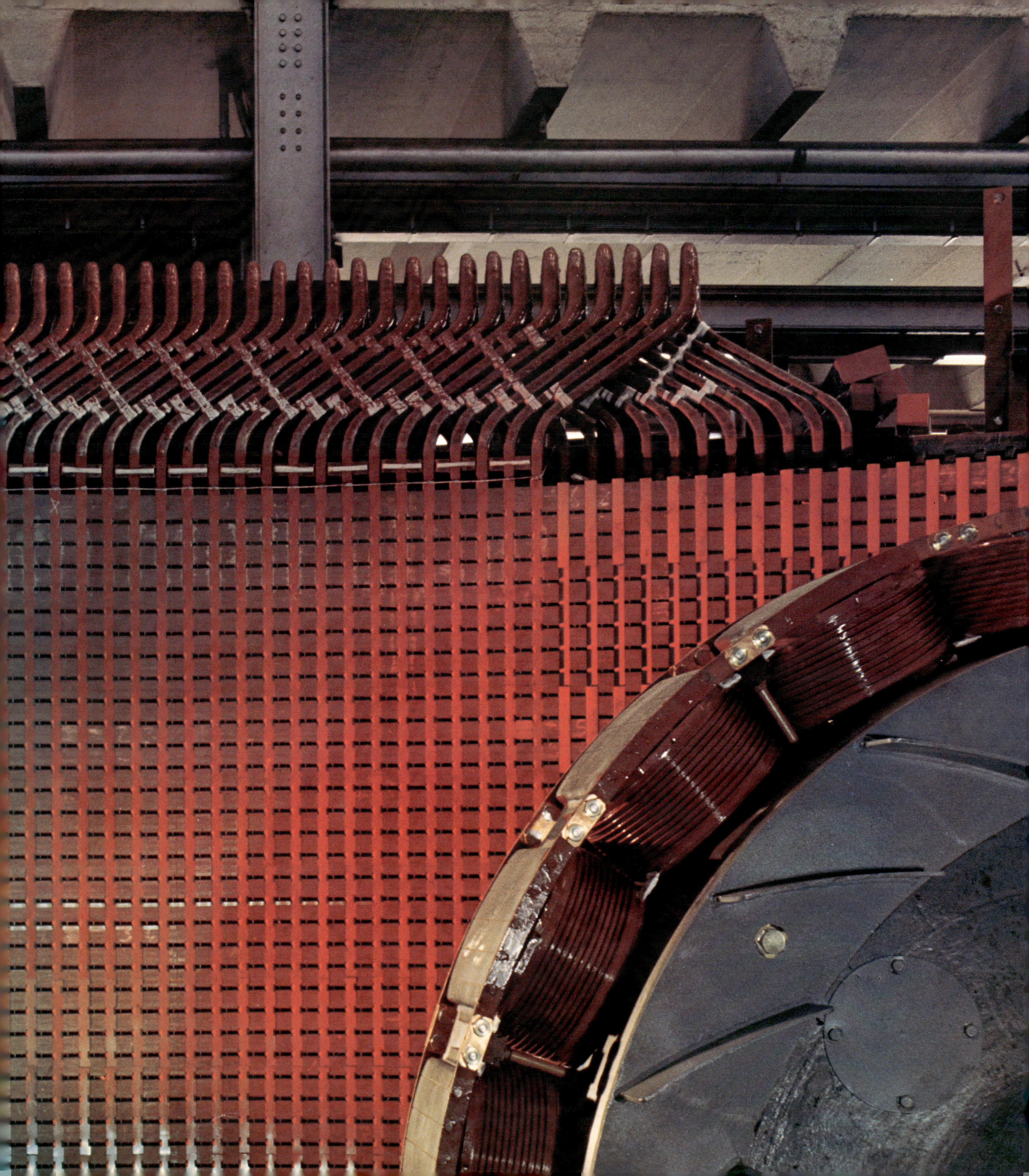

Forschung...

...im Mikrokosmos –
Siemens-Elektronen-
mikroskop

...im Makrokosmos –
Sternwarte
auf dem „Insulaner"

Research...

...in microcosm –
Siemens electronic
microscope

...in macrocosm –
Observatory on Insu-
laner Hill

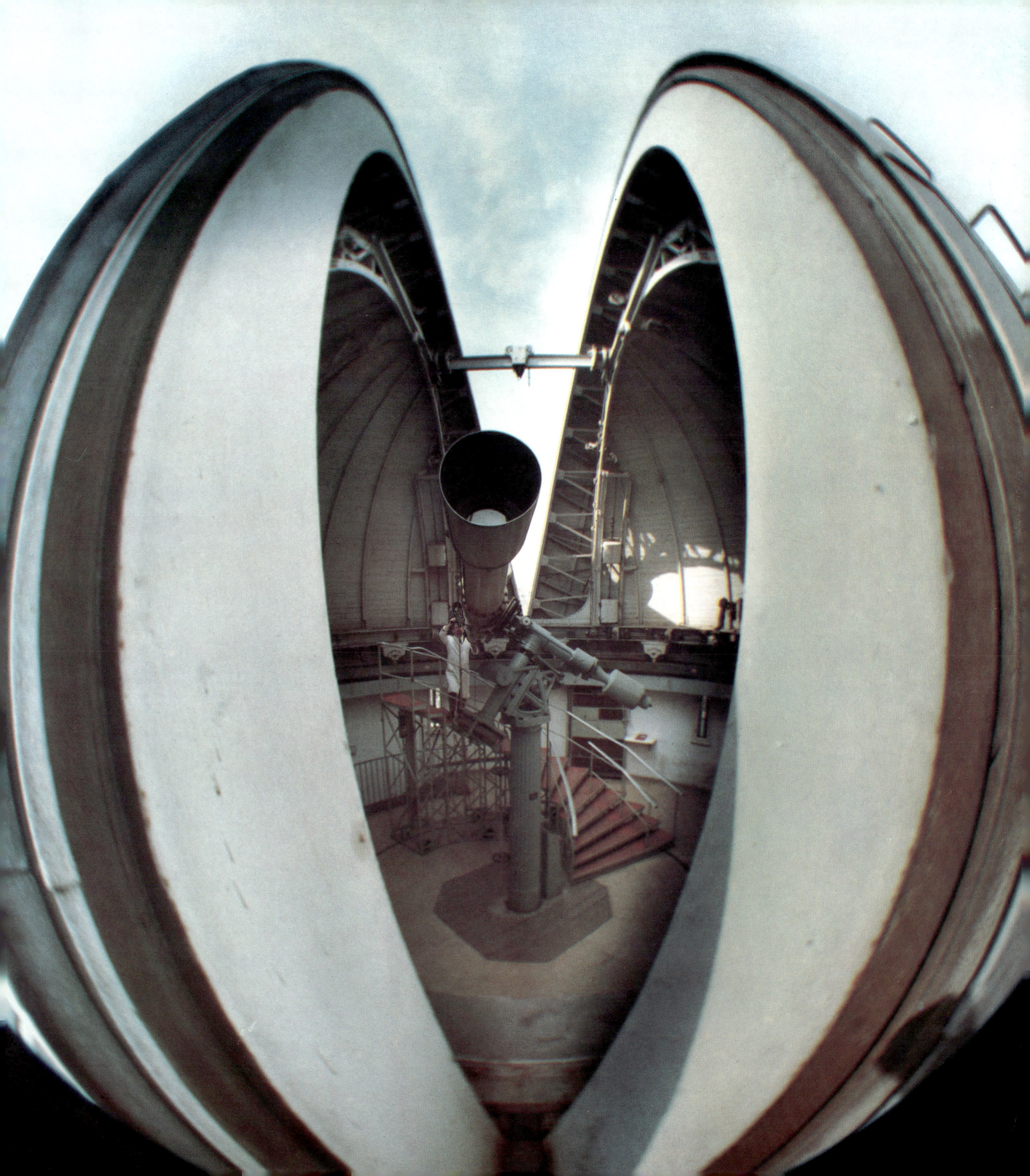

In der Hochschule
für Bildende Künste

In the Academy
of Fine Arts

In der Gipsformerei
der Staatlichen
Museen, Apoll neben
Prinzessin Luise

Plaster casting,
Municipal Museums
Apollo next
to Princess Luise

Zwei Ateliers | Two studios | Heinz Otterson

Ursula Sax

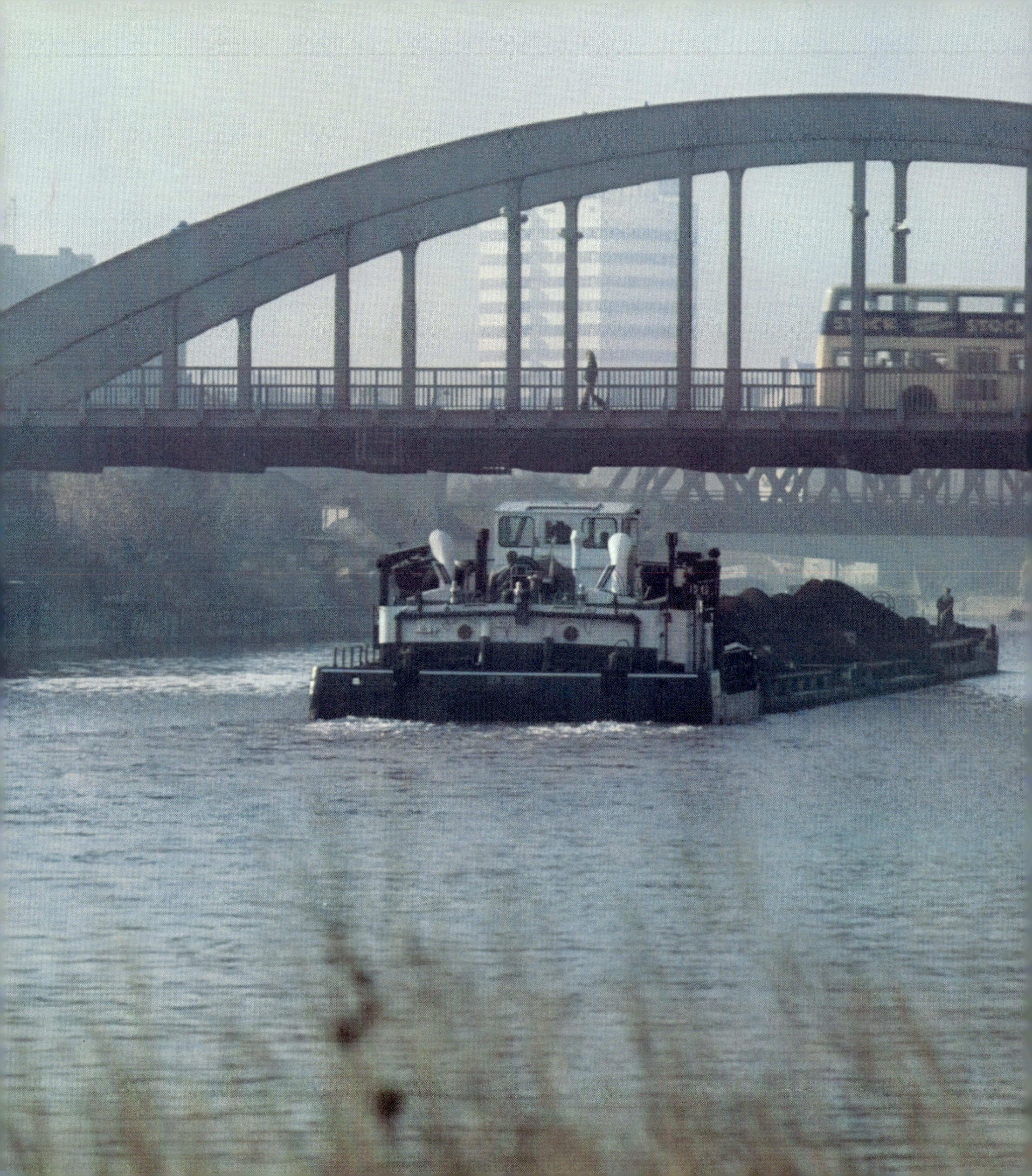
STOCK
STOCK

Spreeschiffer

Boatmen
on the Spree River

Aus alt wird neu...
From old to new...

Schiffsschrottplatz Spandau
Ship junkyard in Spandau

Stahlwerk Borsig
Borsig steel works

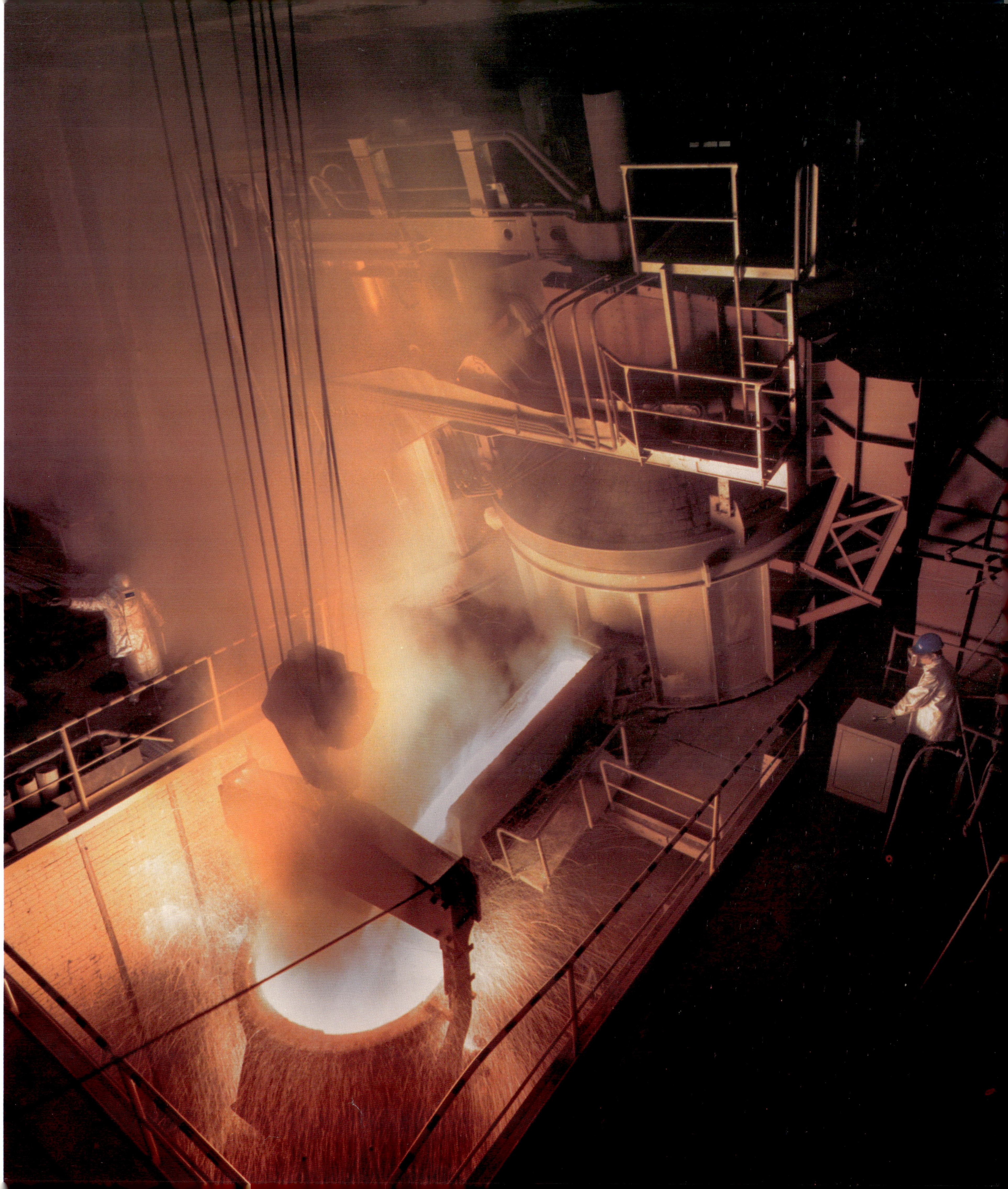

Im übrigen: man arbeitet.	In addition: one works.
Entgegen übler Nachrede	Also, contrary to malicious gossip,
auch an der Freien Universität.	at the Free University.
Mehr als eine Million Erwerbstätige,	Almost half a million wage-earners,
Pro-Kopf-Einkommen des Westberliners	the average income of the West Berliner
9000 Mark im Jahr.	about 9,000 Marks a year.
Das Bruttoinlandsprodukt Westberlins	The gross product of West Berlin exceeds
übertrifft das Schleswig-Holsteins.	that of the whole state of Schleswig-Holstein.
Westberlins Lebensstandard hat,	West Berlin's living standard has,
trotz katastrophaler Startbedingungen,	in spite of catastrophic conditions at the start,
heute das Niveau der Bundesrepublik	today attained the level of the Federal
und der glanzvollsten Städte	Republic and of the most glittering cities
westlicher Zivilisation erreicht.	of western civilization.

Hörsaal
im Klinikum der
Freien Universität
in Steglitz

Classroom
in the Klinikum of
the Free University
in Steglitz

Berlin arbeitet

Berlin at work

Links: Spinnerei Adolff
Mitte: Pharmazeutische Fabrik Schering
Rechts: Schaltwarte im Wasserwerk Tegel

Left: The Adolff spinning mills
Centre: Schering Pharmaceuticals
Right: Switching center Tegel waterworks

Links: Großrechenanlage bei AEG
Mitte: Berliner Porzellan-Manufaktur
Rechts: Zeitungsrotationsmaschine

Left: Computer at AEG
Centre: The Berlin Porcelain Factory
Right: Newspaper printing press

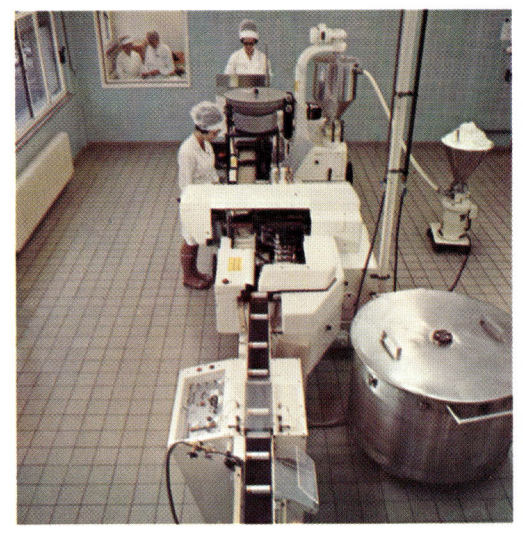

Links: Hochglanz am Ku'damm
Mitte: Wochenmarkt am Rathaus Schöneberg
Rechts: Ambulantes Kunsthandwerk

Left: Kurfürstendamm glitter
Centre: Weekly market at Schöneberg's City Hall
Right: Ambulatory arts and crafts

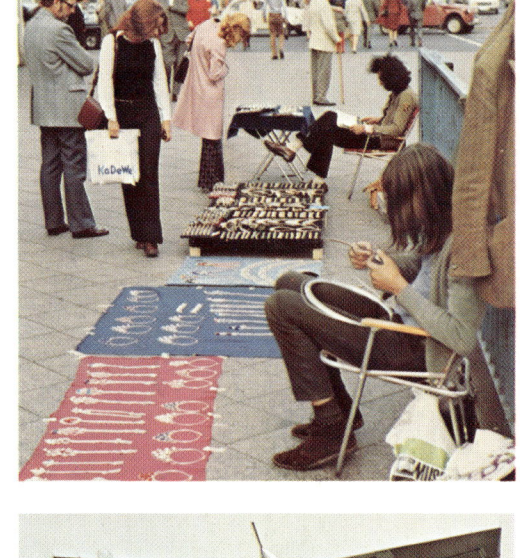

Links: Westhafen mit Zementumschlaganlage
Mitte: Bauer bei Lübars
Rechts: Zentralflughafen Tempelhof

Left: The West Harbor with cementloading landing
Centre: Farmer in Lübars
Right: Tempelhof Central Airport

Blaue Stunde und Nacht

Wird Westberlin immer mehr
ein großes St. Pauli?
Ein Las Vegas im Roten Meer?
Oder ist euer nightlife
ein müder Aufguß
der Goldenen Zwanziger Jahre?

Naja, es gibt keinen Quatsch,
den die Leute nicht glauben.
Erstens, wenn Sie gestatten,
waren die Goldenen Zwanziger
zwar golden, aber nicht echt.
Zugegeben, es ging damals vielerlei los –
vor allem hier in Berlin.
Zwischen Achtzehn und Dreiunddreißig
war Berlin tatsächlich 'ne Drehscheibe
im Zentrum Europas.
Unser Europa-Center ist dagegen
eher rührend, i-Punkt inklusive.
Im übrigen wird viel imitiert.
Klein Las Vegas?
Aber die „einarmigen Diebe" fehlen,
die slotmachines und Spielcasinos
und Franky Sinatras, die Mafia
und die Wüste von Nevada ringsum.
St. Pauli?
Nee, wissen Se, wer Hamburg kennt:
da sind wir nur Waisenknaben.
Unsere horizontalen Damen
wären glücklich,
wenn sie den Umsatz machten.
Striptease hört bei uns noch irgendwo auf.
Sex für alle Lebenslagen,
Klassefrauen, show für Voyeure,
billig, besser und die Extras,
wo fände man das heute nicht –
sogar am Grenzübertritt BRD–Schweiz.
Jazz gibt's in Berlin zwar durchaus,
aber mehr von gastierenden Gruppen,
und dann ist er so gut oder schlecht
wie überall,
internationale Höhepunkte nicht ausgeschlossen.

Nacht über Berlin,
das kann auf andere Weise schöner sein.
Die blaue Stunde, l'heure bleue,
Gottfried Benn hat sie beschrieben,
Dämmerung, Lichter der Großstadt,
in einem Straßen-Café
der Apéritif, die Erwartung,
flanierende Pärchen, auch einzelne Damen,
magische Zauberwelt Schaufenster.
Oder die Eckkneipe: Mief,
Molle mit Korn und Boulette –
„Zum nassen Dreieck",
der beste Platz ist an der Theke,
große Sprüche, kleines Naja.
Die Theater öffnen.
„Haben Sie noch 'n Rang Mitte?"
„Zweimal, bitte."
„Zauberflöte" oder „Biografie" von Frisch?
Danach noch ein Gläschen.
Kempinski, Die Spitze,
oder oben bei Conrad Hilton am Rundkamin,
Panoramablick von fast nach Manhattan
bis fast nach Sibirien –
as you like it – carajo.
Vielleicht, wenn der Sinn so steht,
dann doch noch ins Cheetah,
Chez Nous, New Eden oder Leydicke.
Aber der Sound im Big Apple
wird schließlich zu laut,
das letzte Schultheiß steht schal,
zahlen, wir gehen.
In Berlin kann eben,
sagte schon Friedrich der Große,
jeder nach seiner Façon selig werden.
Die Nacht ist lau,
im Tiergarten flüstern die Blätter
der nachgewachsenen Bäume,
und die nachgewachsenen Liebespaare auch.
Überm Tor, dem Brandenburger,
an der Quadriga befestigt,
die unbeirrt ostwärts blickt –
hängt eine Fahne, angestrahlt, demonstrativ,
gleichgültig, träge, ohne Bewegung:
schwarz-rot-gold.

The "Blue Hour" and Night

Has West Berlin become ever more
a larger version of Hamburg's rowdy St. Pauli?
A Las Vegas in the Red Sea?
Or is its nightlife
a tired infusion
out of the Golden Twenties?

Well – yes; no story's too silly
for people not to believe it.
To start with, if you'll allow me,
the Golden Twenties
may have been gold, but not genuine.
Conceded, plenty went on then,
especially here in Berlin.
Between 1918 and 1933
Berlin truly was a turntable
in the center of Europe.
Our Europa-Center is by comparison a bit
touching, even including the "i-Punkt"
In addition, much is imitation.
Little Las Vegas?
But the one-armed bandits are missing,
the slot-machines and the gambling casinos
and Frank Sinatras, the Mafia
and the surrounding desert of Nevada.
St. Pauli?
Ah, no; anyone who knows Hamburg knows
that we're just a poor relation.
Our horizontal ladies
would be happy to have
such a turn-over.
Striptease
here still stops at one point or another.
Sex for all walks of life,
terrific girls, shows for voyeurs,
cheap, better, with all the extras –
where can you not find that today?
Even at West Germany's Swiss border.

Of jazz you can find a plenty in Berlin,
but mostly by visiting groups,
and it's then just as good or bad
as anywhere,
not excluding international high points.
Night in Berlin,
that can be more enjoyable in other ways.
The blue hour, l'heure bleue
(Gottfried Benn has described it),
twilight, lights of the great city,
in a sidewalk café
the apéritif, the expectation,
strolling couples, also ladies alone,
magic world of show-windows.
Or the corner bar: heavy air,
beer with schnapps and snacks:
"Zum nassen Dreieck" – "At the Fluid Triangle" –
the best place is at the counter,
big opinions, small "Well – yes."
The theaters open."One left in the center balcony?"
"Two, please."
Magic Flute or Max Frisch's Biography?
And after that a drink.
The Kempinski's bar, or Die Spitze,
or up at Conrad Hilton's round fireplace,
panoramic view almost from Manhattan
almost to Siberia –
as you like it – carajo.
Perhaps, if that's your taste,
on to the Cheetah,
Chez Nous, the New Eden, or Leydicke's.
But the beat at the Big Apple
finally grows too loud,
the last beer grows stale,
"Check, please", and then off.
In Berlin, when you come down to it,
as Frederick the Great put it,
everyone can find happiness in his own way.
The night is balmy,
in the Tiergarten rustle the leaves
of the re-planted trees –
the re-planted loving couples, too.
Up above, on the Brandenburg Gate,
hoisted over the Quadriga
which looks imperturbably eastward,
hangs a flag, illuminated, demonstrative,
indifferent, sluggish, immobile:
black-red-gold.

Kurfürstendamm

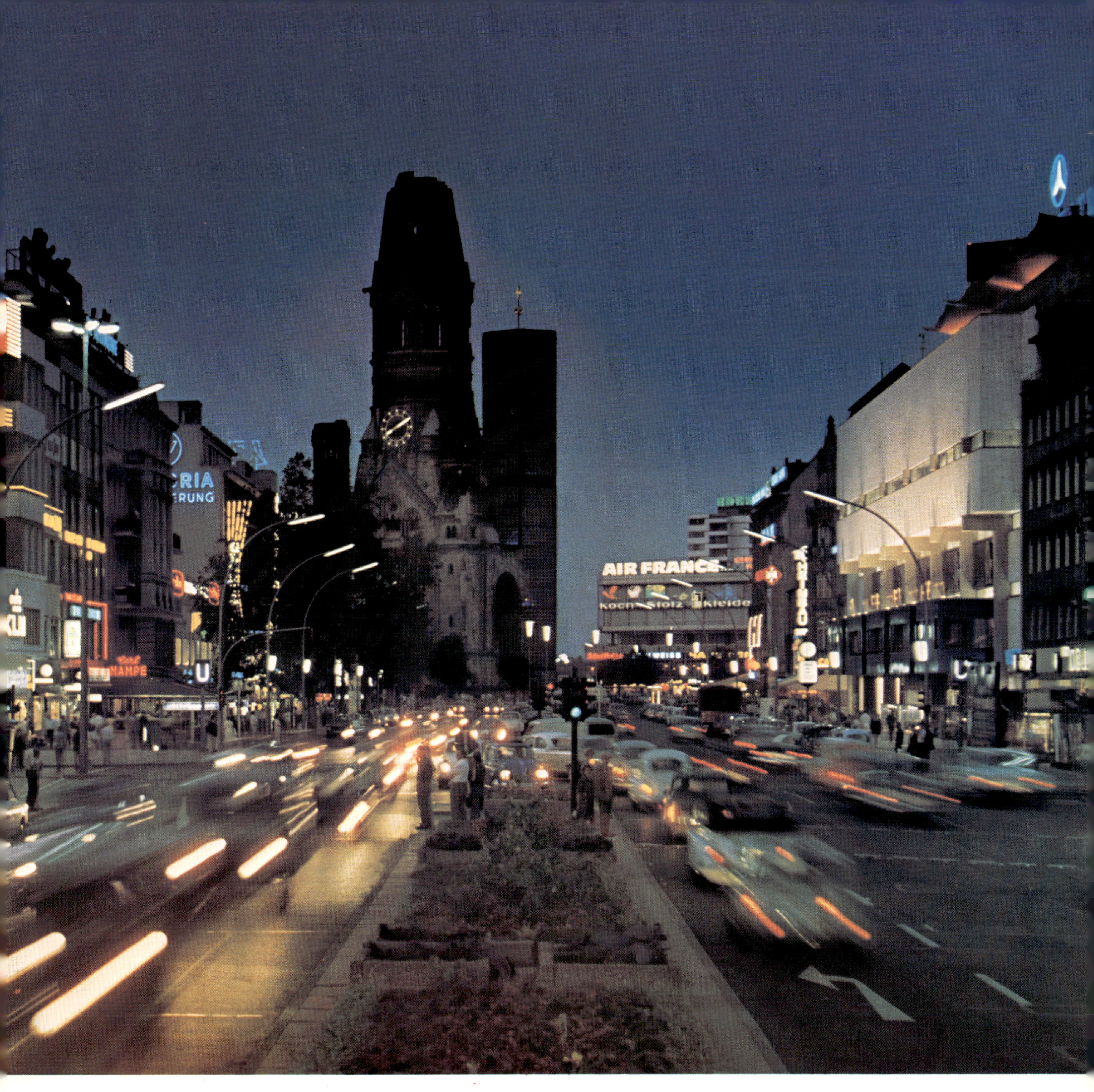
AIR FRANCE
Koch Stolz Kleider
MAMPE
U

Platz der Republik vor dem Reichstag – „Symposion europäischer Bildhauer" 1961–63

"Platz der Republik" before the Reichstag – "Symposium of European Sculptors" 1961–63

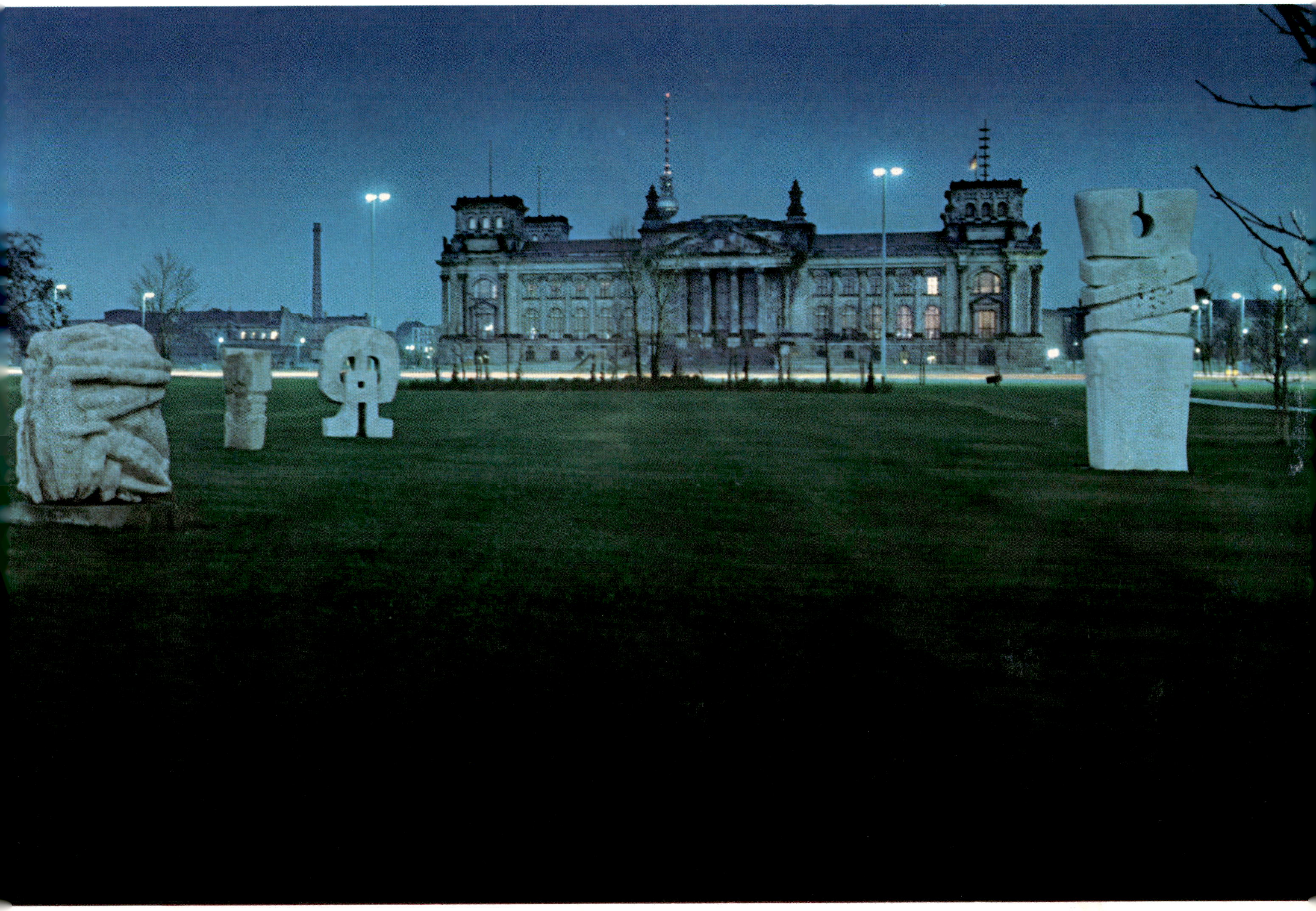

Schaufenster... ...Trödel
Show – windows... „rechts vom Ku'damm"
...second-hand shops off the Kurfürstendamm

... den Ku'damm
auf und ab

... show-windows
along the
Kurfürstendamm

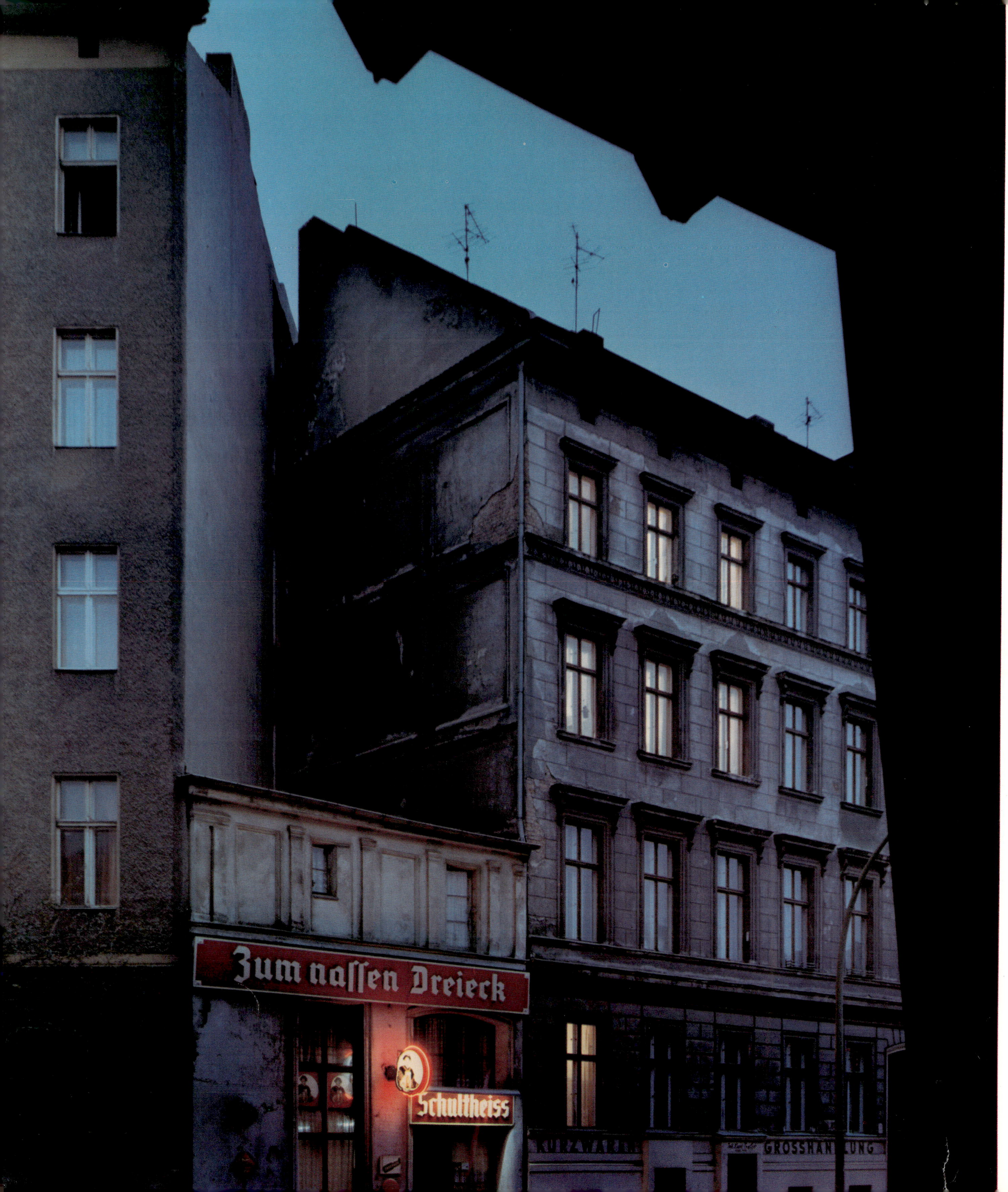
Zum naſſen Dreieck
Schultheiss

Kneipen –
für 'ne Molle und 'n Korn
mit Hackepeter
oder Boulette

Kneipen
Berlin bars
for a beer
and a schnapps
and a snack

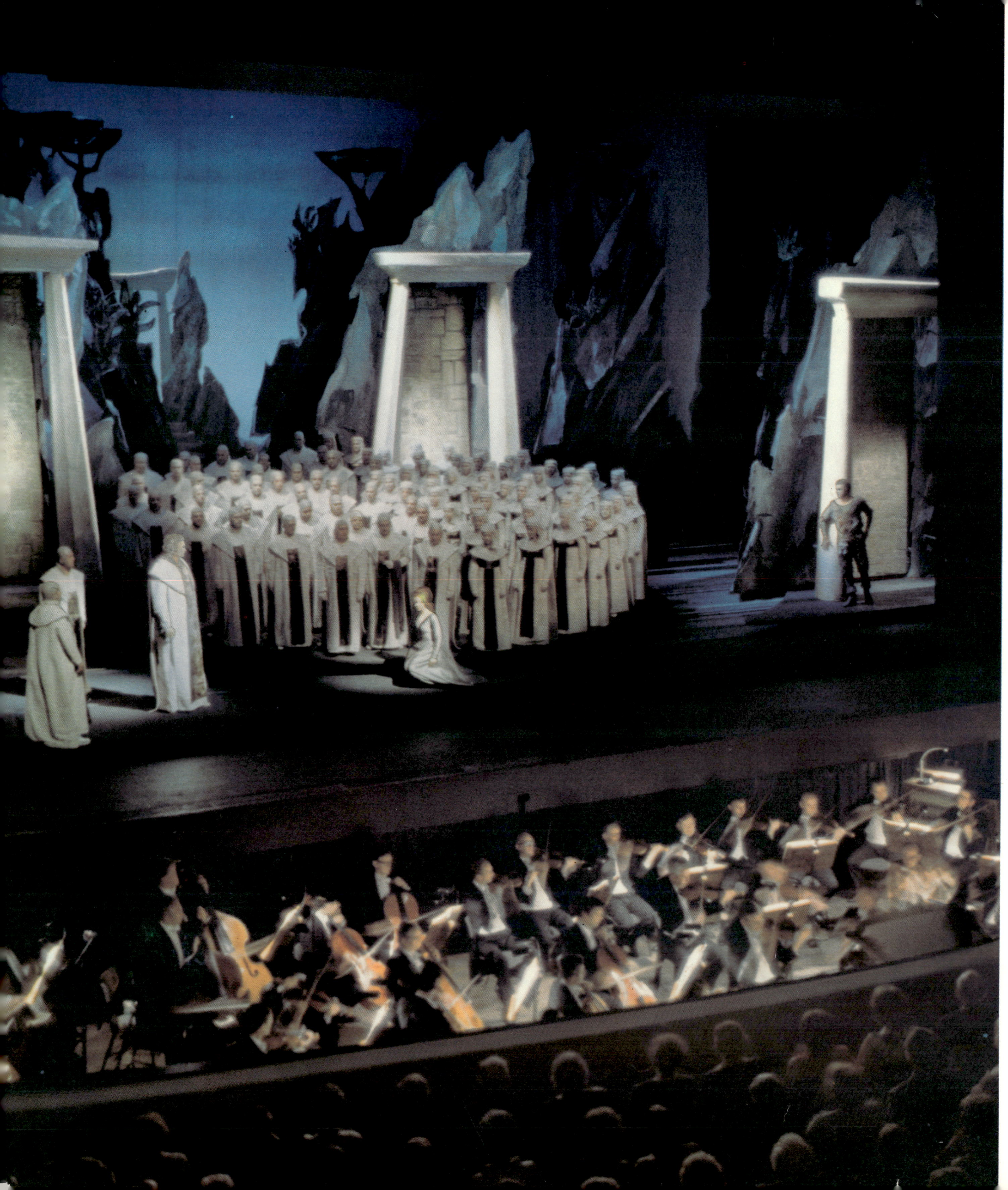

Musik...

...in der
Deutschen Oper
„Zauberflöte" –

...im 'Leierkasten'
Jazz

Music...

...The Magic Flute
in the Deutsche
Oper Berlin

...Jazz in the
"Leierkasten" bar

„Jazz in the garden"
Skulpturenhof
der Neuen
Nationalgalerie

"Jazz in the garden"
Sculpture Court
of the
New National Gallery

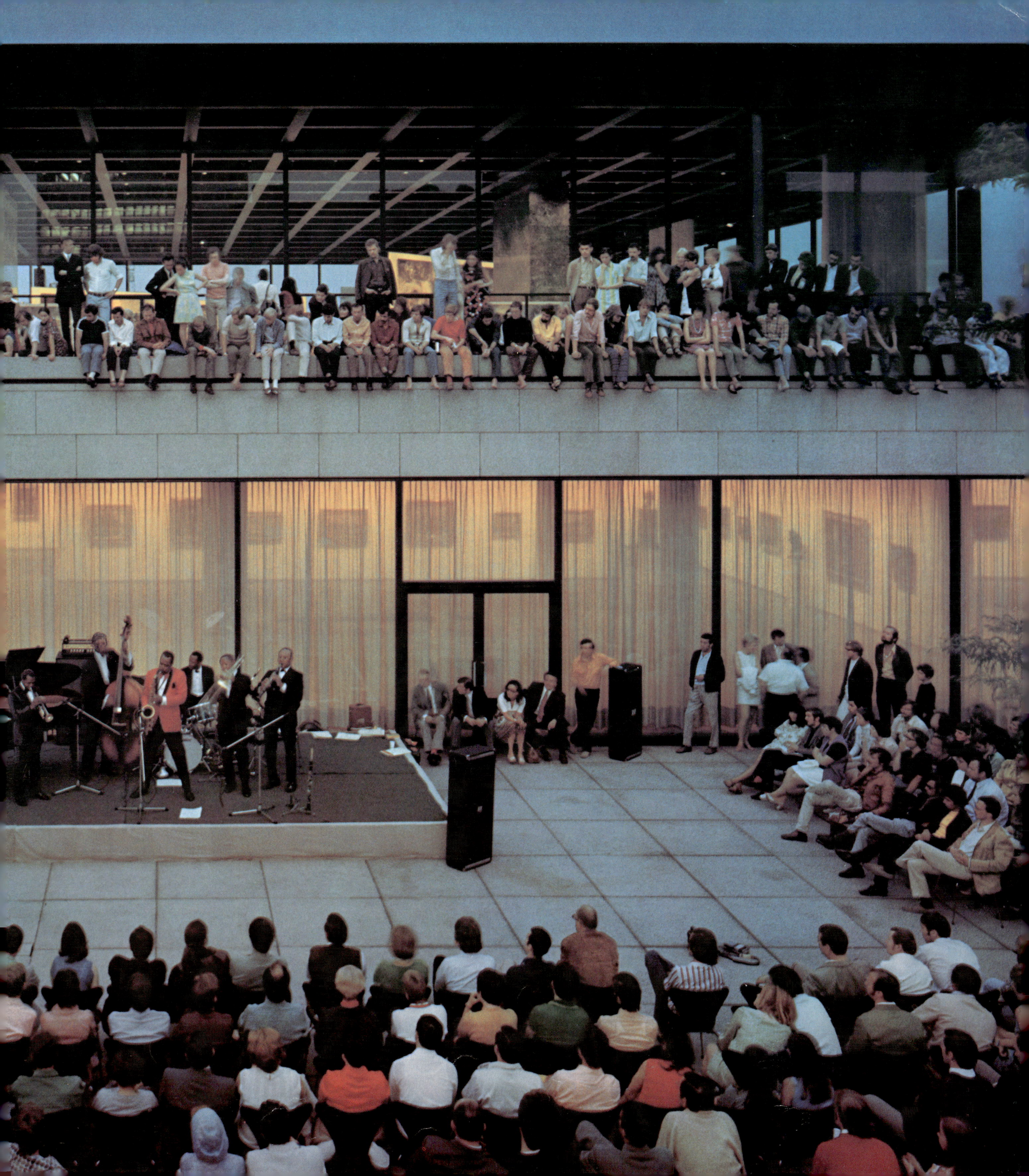

Popmusik
aus zwei Welten:

Leierkastenmann
in Berlin-N

'Cheetah'
der Beatschuppen
in Edelstahl

Pop music
from two worlds:

Organ-grinder
in northern Berlin

"Cheetah"
stainless steel
discothèque

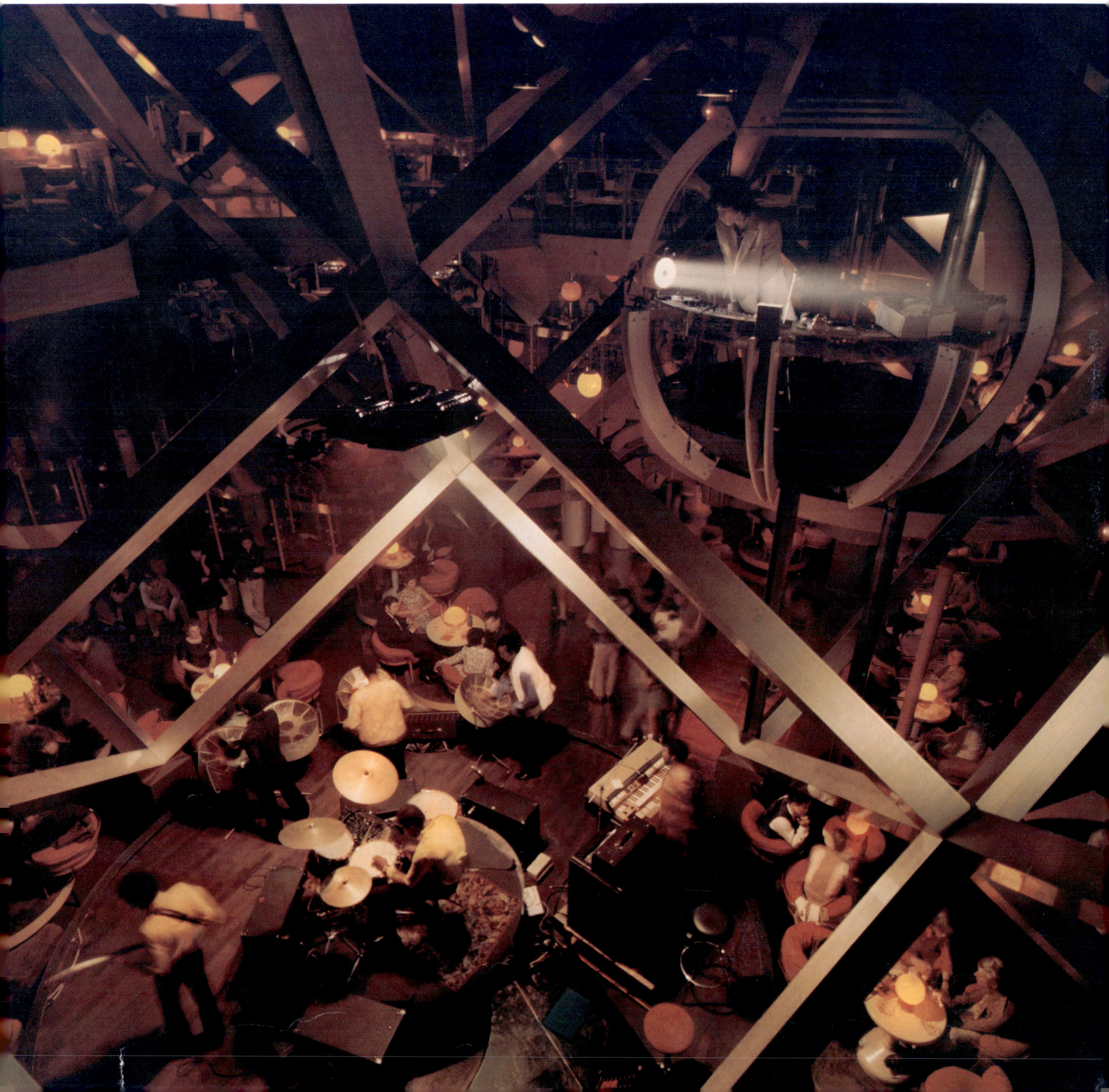

Sex

Im 'Shoppop'
In the "Shoppop"

Im 'Daily Girl'

In "The Daily Girl"

'Leydicke' in Kreuzberg

"Leydicke" in Kreuzberg

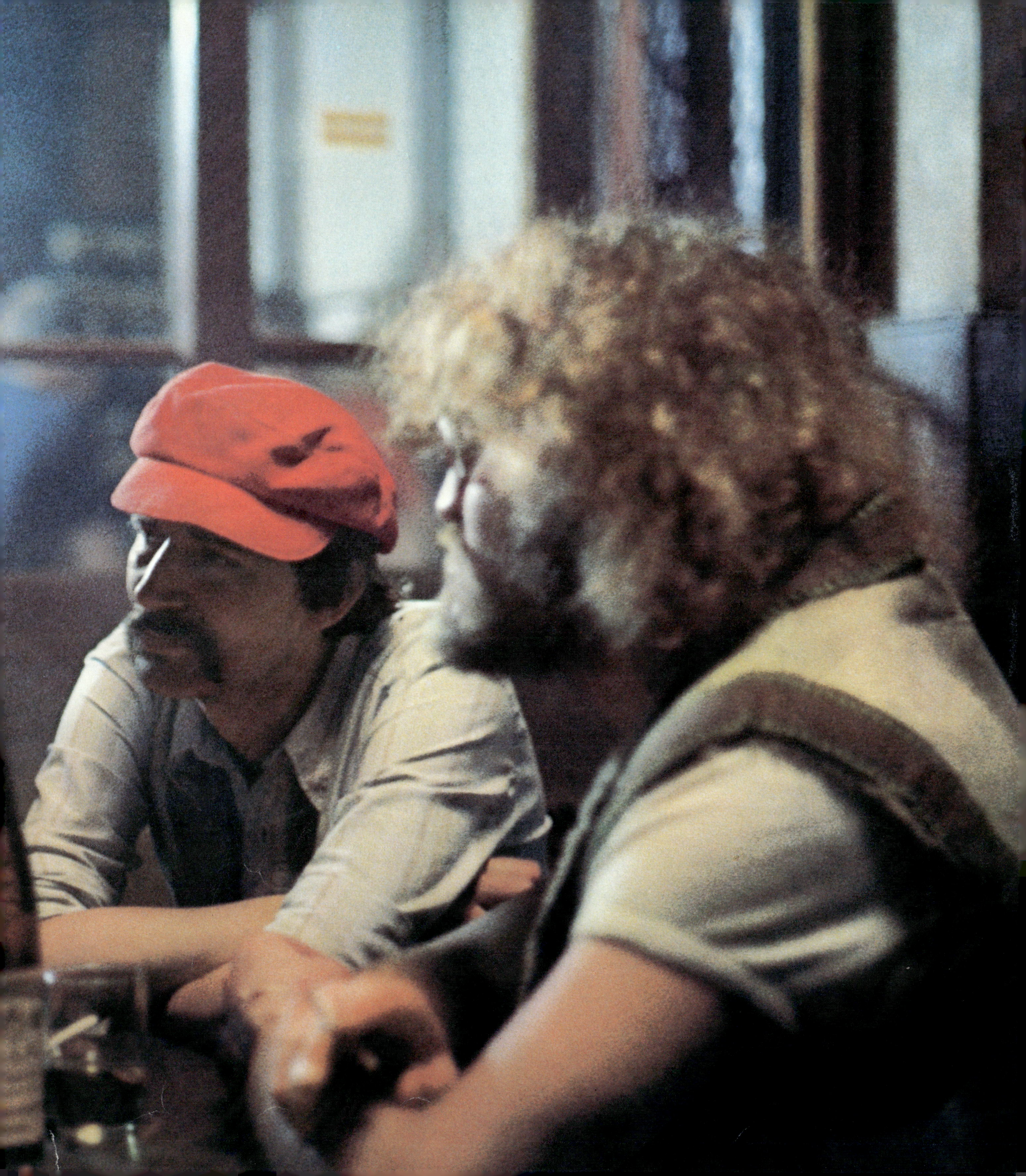

Im 'Chez nous'
(... denn die Damen
das sind Herren ...)

At the "Chez Nous"
(... where the ladies
are actually
gentlemen ...)

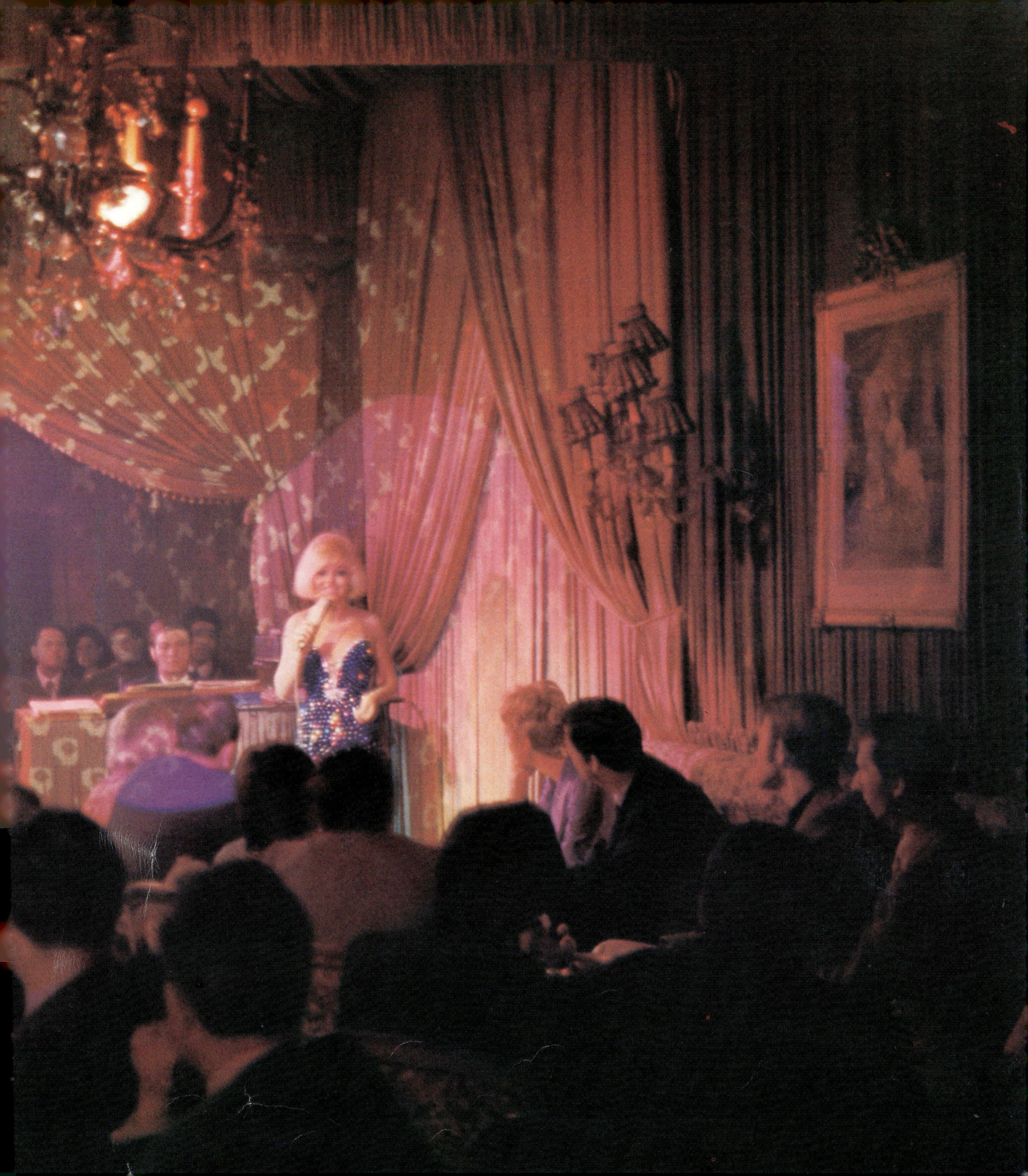

Beat
im 'Big Apple'

Beat
at the "Big Apple"

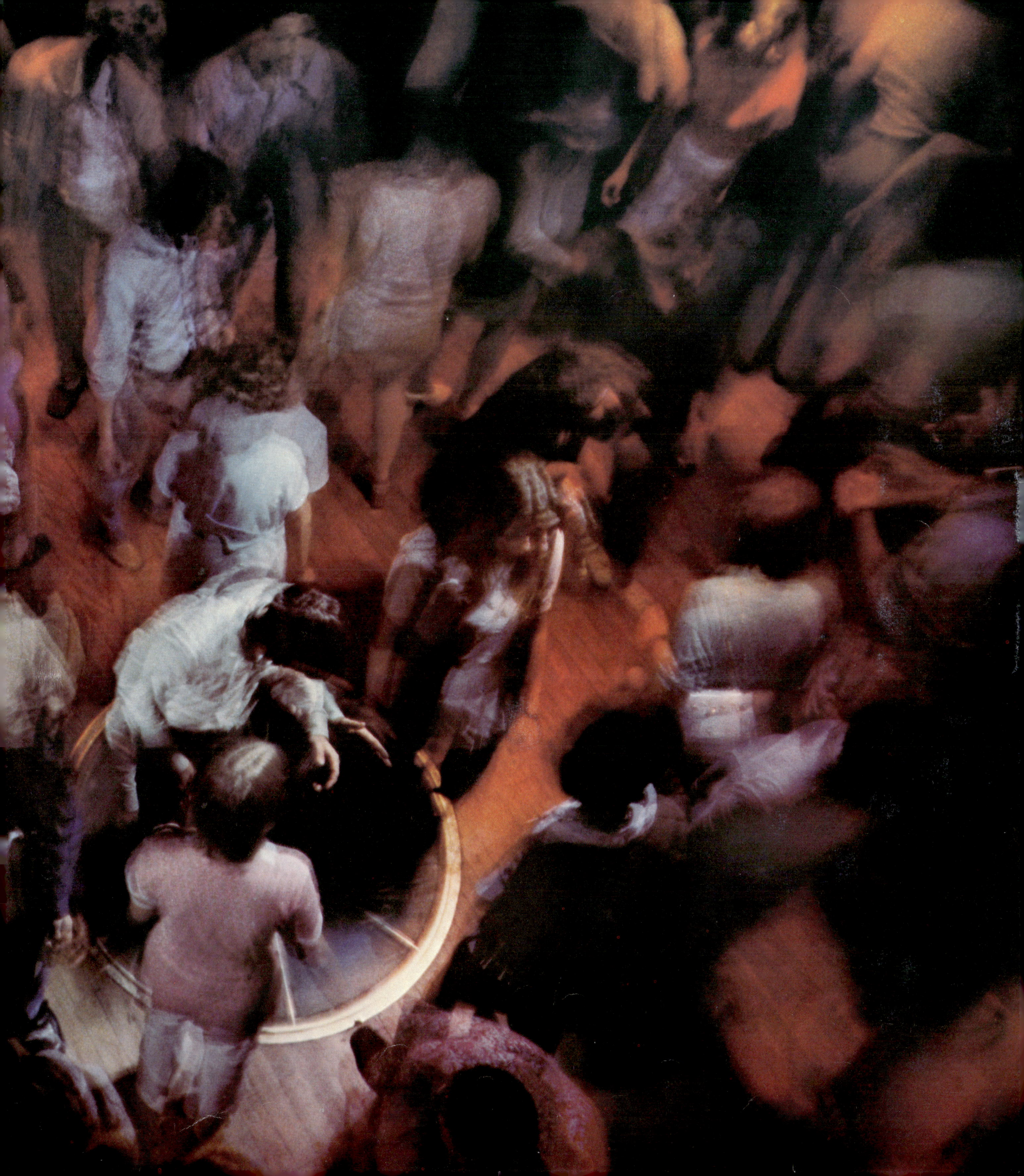

Sperlingsgasse, bombenzerstört,
wie fast das ganze Alt-Berlin.
Wilhelm Raabe schrieb dort als Student
sein erstes Buch.
Heute: ein künstlicher Abglanz
bei Nacht, für Touristen in Westberlin.
Aber Berlin ist kein Museum,
Hunderttausende junger Leute –
die Bevölkerungspyramide gesundet –
wissen ganz gut, wo in Berlin
sie am Abend das finden,
was sie suchen. Zum Beispiel:
„sich schaffen", beim Beat.

The Sperlingsgasse, bombed out
like most of the rest of old Berlin.
Wilhelm Raabe as a student
wrote his first book there.
Today: an artificial bit of reflected splendor
by night, for tourists, in West Berlin.
But Berlin is no museum;
hundreds of thousands of young people
(the population pyramid grows healthier)
know very well where in Berlin
they can find in the evening
what they seek. For instance:
a hard rock workout.

Sperlingsgasse –
alles
„echt imitiert"

Sperlingsgasse –
everything
"genuine imitation"

Was machen Sie abends?

What are you doing this evening?

Links: Schillertheater
Mitte: Deutsche Oper, Ballett
Rechts: Im Kabarett „Die Stachelschweine"

Left: The Schiller Theater
Centre: The Deutsche Oper Berlin, ballet
Right: "Die Stachelschweine" satirical cabaret

Links: 'Galerie Natubs' Treffpunkt für junge Leute
Mitte: Jazz in der 'Eierschale'
Rechts: Foyer der „Schaubühne am Halleschen Ufer"

Left: The "Natubs Gallery" a meeting-place for young people
Centre: Jazz at the "Eierschale"
Right: Lobby of the "Schaubühne am Halleschen Ufer"

Links: Presseball im Palais am Funkturm
Mitte: 'Ballhaus Resi'
Rechts: Reit- und Springturnier in der Deutschlandhalle

Left: The Press Ball in the Palais am Funkturm
Centre: "Ballhaus Resi"
Right: Equestrian tournament in the Deutschlandhalle

Links: Transvestitenshow im 'Chez nous'
Mitte: Go-Go-Girls im 'Playboy-Club'
Rechts: Pool im 'Eden'

Left: Transvestite show at the "Chez Nous"
Centre: Go-go girls at the "Playboy Club"
Right: Pool at the "Eden"

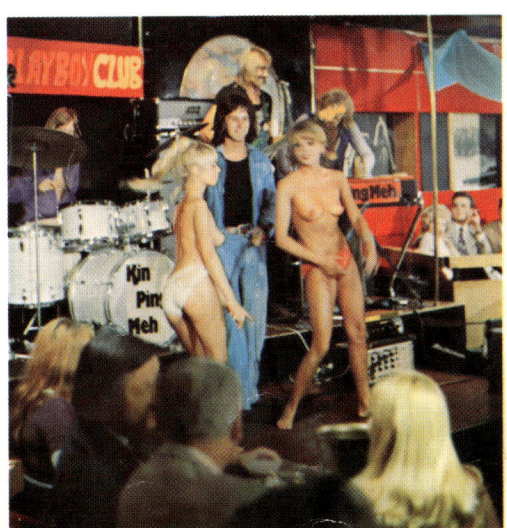

Das Tor

Siebzehnhunderteinundneunzig:
Das Tor kann pünktlich eingeweiht werden,
weil die schöne Wilhelmine,
Tochter des Regimentstrompeters Enke,
Mätresse Friedrich Wilhelms II.,
energisch die Bauaufsicht führte.
Achtzehnhundertundsieben:
Durch die Säulen von Langhans
zieht Napoleon Bonaparte als Sieger,
raubt Schadows Quadriga.
Sieben Jahre später holen die Preußen
das Rössergespann zurück aus Paris.
Im Biedermeier flanieren hier
Dandies und junge Damen,
Heine: „Grüß mich nicht unter den Linden".
Achtzehnhundertachtundvierzig:
Die Revolution wird niederkartätscht,
der König grüßt die schwarz-rot-goldene Fahne.
Fünfundfünfzig: die erste Pferdebahn rollt.
Achtzehnhundertsiebzig: Menzel malt
vor'm Tor die Abreise Wilhelms nach Frankreich.
Mit klingendem Spiel ziehen später
die Sieger von Sedan hier ein.
Achtundsiebzig: Berliner Kongreß,
Bismarck als ehrlicher Makler,
sein Deutsches Reich will den Frieden Europas.
Neunzehnhundertundvierzehn:
„Unsere Feldgrauen" rücken aus.
Achtzehn, neunzehn, zwanzig:
Wilhelm II. verläßt für immer Berlin,
Liebknecht verkündet die Revolution.
Fünfundzwanzig: Trauerfahnen für Ebert,
Hindenburg wird gefeiert.
Neunundzwanzig: letztes Geleit für Stresemann.
Neunzehnhundertdreiunddreißig:
größter Fackelzug aller Zeiten,
Hakenkreuzfahne auf der Quadriga.
Sechsunddreißig: Feuerwerk, Olympiade –
die Welt zu Gast im braunen Berlin.
Vierzig: Sieg über Frankreich, Parade,
später die Bombennächte.
Fünfundvierzig: Schlacht um Berlin,
Sowjetsoldaten heften die rote Fahne
an die Quadriga.
Dreiundfünfzig: Berliner Arbeiter holen
die Fahne herunter, verbrennen sie: 17. Juni.
Einundsechzig: die Mauer am 13. 8.
Zweiundsiebzig: Viermächteabkommen,
Gewaltverzicht – Wandel durch Annäherung?

The Gate

Seventeen hundred and ninety-one:
the dedication of the gate
could take place on time
because beautiful Wilhelmine,
daughter of the regiment's Trumpeter Enke,
mistress of Friedrich Wilhelm II,
energetically supervised the construction work.
Eighteen hundred and seven:
through Langhans' columns
passes Napoleon Bonaparte the victor,
and steals Schadow's Quadriga.
Seven years later the Prussians fetch
their team of horses back from Paris.
Here stroll during the Biedermeier period
dandies and young ladies;
Heinrich Heine: "Unter den Linden, greet me not."
Eighteen hundred and forty-eight:
the revolution is mowed down,
the King salutes the black-red-golden flag.
1855: the first horse-drawn car rolls.
1870: Menzel paints, with the Gate as background,
Wilhelm's departure against France.
Later, to the ring of martial music,
the victors of Sedan pass through here.
1878: the Congress of Berlin,
Bismarck as "the honest broker",
his German Empire seeking peace in Europe.
Nineteen hundred and fourteen:
our troops in battle dress move out.
1918, '19, '20:
Kaiser Wilhelm II leaves Berlin forever,
Karl Liebknecht proclaims the revolution.
'25: mourning for Friedrich Ebert,
celebrations for Hindenburg.
'29: Stresemann laid to rest.
Nineteen hundred and thirty-three:
the biggest torchlight parade of all time,
swastika flag on the Quadriga.
'36: fireworks, the Olympics,
the world pays a visit to brown Berlin.
'40: victory over France, parade,
followed by nights of bombs.
'45: the Battle of Berlin,
Soviet soldiers hoist the red flag
on the Quadriga.
'53: Berlin workers pull
that flag down, burn it: June 17th.
'61: the Wall on August 13th.
'72: Four-power Agreement, relaxation of tensions
change through rapprochement?

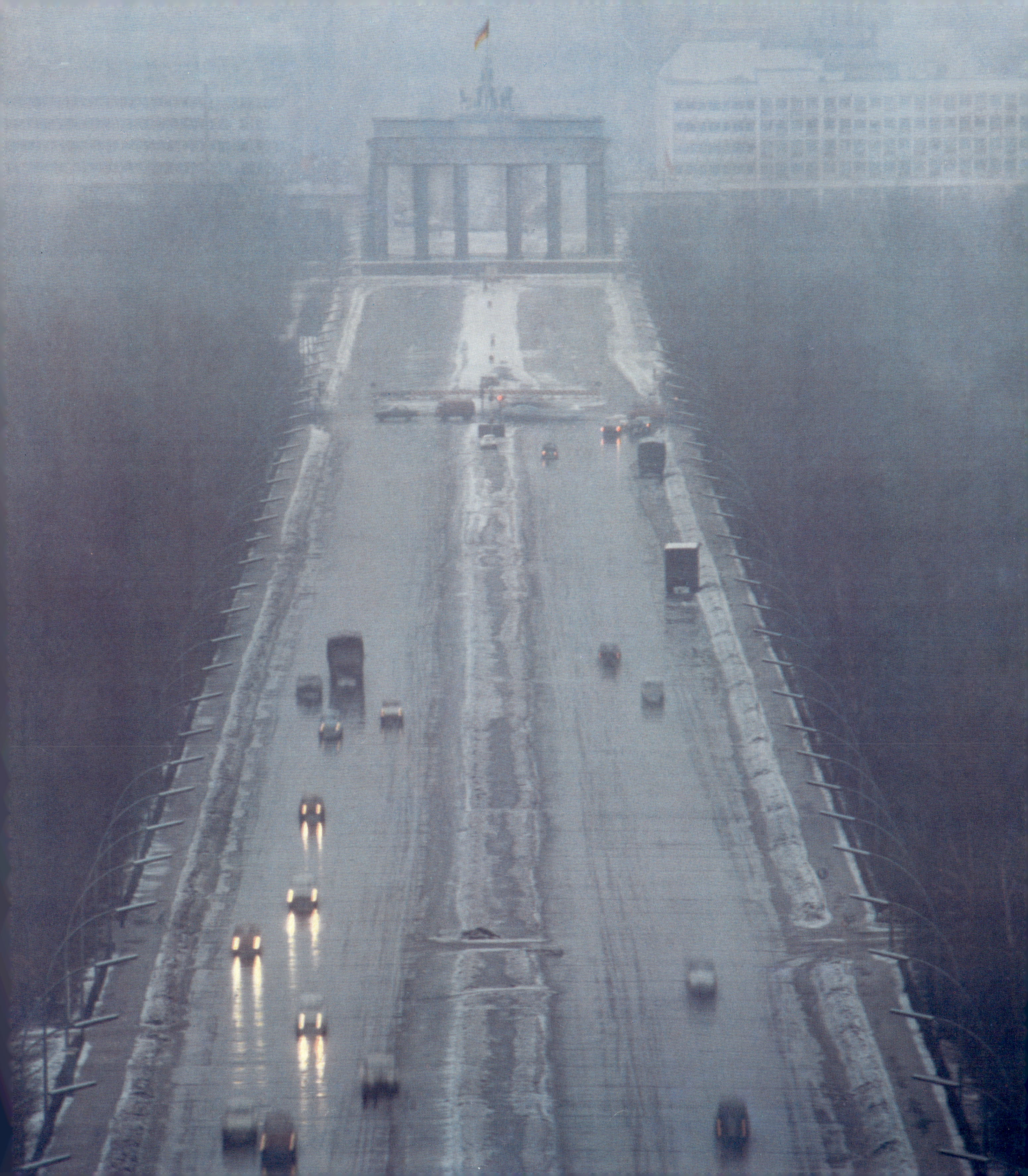

Prière de ne pas quitter le passage

Blick nach Westen
von der „i-Punkt"-
Fernrohrterrasse
auf dem
Europa-Center

View westward
from the "i-Punkt"
telescope row
atop the
Europa-Center

Ludwig Windstoßer dankt allen,
die ihm halfen, indirekt und direkt:
Passanten, Hausmeister, Arbeiter, Leierkastenmänner,
Kinder, Künstler, verliebte Paare, Taxichauffeure,
alte Damen, junge Damen,
Museumswärter, Pastoren, Direktoren und Senatoren
(und deren Zerberusse), Männer und Frauen
in Kneipen, Schlössern und auf den Straßen Berlins.
Vor allem aber dankt Ludwig Windstoßer:
seiner Assistentin Regina
und seinem Freunde Ben Wargin.

Ludwig Windstoßer thanks all those
who helped him, indirectly and directly:
passers-by, caretakers, workmen, organ-grinders,
children, artists, loving couples, taxi-drivers,
old ladies, young ladies,
museum attendants, pastors, directors, senators
(and their Cerberuses), men and women
in bars, palaces, and on Berlin's streets.
But most of all Ludwig Windstoßer thanks:
his assistant Regina
and his friend Ben Wargin.